If White Kids Die

Dick J. Reavis

University of North Texas Press
Denton, Texas

10 9 8 7 6 5 4 3 2 1

Permissions:
University of North Texas Press
PO Box 311336
Denton TX 76203-1336

The paper used in this book meets the minimum requirements of the American National Standard for Permanence of Paper for Printed Library Materials, z39.48.1984. Binding materials have been chosen for durability.

Library of Congress Cataloging-in-Publication Data
Reavis, Dick J.
    If white kids die : memories of a civil rights movement volunteer / Dick J. Reavis.— 1st ed.
        p.   cm.
Includes index.
    ISBN 1-57441-129-2 (alk. paper)
    1. Reavis, Dick J. 2. Civil rights workers—Alabama—Demopolis—Biography. 3. Whites—United States—Biography. 4. Southern Christian Leadership Conference—History. 5. African Americans—Suffrage—Alabama—Demopolis—History—20th century. 6. African Americans—Civil rights—Alabama—Demopolis—History—20th century. 7. Demopolis (Ala.)—Race relations. 8. Civil rights movements—Alabama—Demopolis—History—20th century. I. Title.
    F334.D3 R43 2001
    323.1'1960730761392—dc21   00-012904

Design by Angela Schmitt

To Charlie Saulsberry, wherever he might be.

CONTENTS

PREFACE

I AM A WHITE TEXAS MALE, now of middle age. Thirty-five years ago, during the summers of 1965 and 1966, I was a civil rights worker in Alabama. My part in what we called the Movement was small. I didn't set policy or appear on TV. I did my time in the ranks, got out when I felt I should, and tried for years, without much success, to put the Movement behind me.

As the years have passed, I have watched as, in my recollections, I have diminished from hero to martyr to just a kid who was there. With every diminution, the present has become easier to face.

I was a young man with an uncertain future when I joined the Movement. I was a young man conscious of my destiny when I came out. The Movement didn't make me whatever I am today, any more than the Vietnam War made its veterans whatever they are. But it wasn't a passing fascination, either.

What I saw in one small ghetto left me enraged for twenty years. Not until the mid eighties could I begin to assess my experiences in a cold light. Though I'm a journalist, I didn't write what I had begun to understand even then, because I knew that I couldn't give the tale the dramatic structure that the longer forms of journalism require. All I could do was write a simple memoir, and professionally speaking, there was no point in that.

Now it seems that there's no point in doing anything less, or anything else. But the story that I will tell has been corroded by time. I clearly remember names, words, and ideas that came to me by ear; my memory of visual elements is much less reliable, and the sequence of some events now confuses me. While writing, I worried for weeks about some of these elements, and tried to contact people whose spots of memory might complement mine. But the Movement's people have scattered and died. On top of that, the only figures who could have spoken authoritatively about developments that were a mystery on the black side of the color line, the handful of moderate whites in Demopolis, have mostly died or been laid low by Alzheimer's.

The story of the civil rights movement as I knew it has not been told, perhaps because it does not end with the lofty victories that are officially commemorated today. The Movement's incomplete struggle will probably not be resumed during my lifetime, though someday, I'm sure it will, because at bottom, it wasn't about color, anyway: it was about human equality, the oldest cause known to man. It is my hope that this work will help place the Southern civil rights struggle in a broader and more realistic context.

Dallas, 1998
Austin, 1999
San Antonio, 2000

Chapter 1

I GOT INTO THE SOUTHERN civil rights movement, I believe, thanks to the mistake of a mailing room clerk. During the spring of 1965, I was a student at a small Oklahoma school, Panhandle A&M College, a place known for its rodeo team and the motto inscribed on the marker at its entrance, "Progress Thru Education."

I had gone there because, during my first three semesters in college, I had done poorly at a state university in my home state of Texas.

One afternoon I stepped into the Panhandle student union cafeteria to grab a glass of iced tea, and if I recall rightly, to lay eyes on Annette, a black co-ed whom I was secretly dating. She worked at the Union in the afternoons.

Lying on the table where I took a seat was a brochure whose purpose was to recruit students for summer civil rights duty in the Deep South. It wasn't supposed to be there. Panhandle wasn't the place for it. Reed College, it was not. Its students, mostly whites from farming towns, many of whom came to college to study agriculture, weren't those that civil rights organizations were making an effort to court.

The summer of 1964 had been "Freedom Summer" for a few campuses. The most militant civil rights group, SNCC, the misnamed Student Non-Violent Co-Ordinating Committee, had drawn some 500 mostly white students from Ivy League and prestige liberal universities to help its integration efforts in Mississippi. White Boston Congressman Barney Frank, today known as an advocate of gay liberation, was one of those who went South for the SNCC (pronounced 'SNICK') crusade.

SNCC's purpose in organizing the whites was unknown to me at the time. In 1964, an up-and-coming leader named Stokely Carmichael had told a group of prospective volunteers in New York that SNCC wanted to be sure that if blacks were killed on Movement duty, whites would die with them. The demise of kids from the nation's Harvards and Yales, he'd said, would attract press attention to the brutalities of Jim Crow. That wasn't the only reason that SNCC wanted whites, perhaps, but what Stokely said was absolutely prophetic, even if it wasn't popular. A few weeks after his speech, three figures were murdered by Ku Kluxers in Philadelphia, Mississippi: Michael Schwerner, twenty-four, a white Congress of Racial Equality (CORE) staffer from Brooklyn, Cornell, and Columbia; Andrew Goodman, twenty, another white New Yorker, from Queens College, a Freedom Summer volunteer; and a Mississippi African-American plasterer and CORE agitator James Chaney, twenty-one. The press and most of the nation were scandalized.

In March 1965, Mrs. Viola Liuzzo, a white Detroit housewife, had been murdered during the Selma campaign, while working with Dr. Martin Luther King Jr's Southern Christian Leadership Conference (SCLC). Again the press, and with it most of the nation, was enraged. Her death confirmed that whites were useful as martyrs, even if we didn't have Ivy League credentials. Perhaps the bulletin I found at Panhandle was mailed to all colleges, thanks to her martyrdom, but I doubt that the Movement had the resources to make a blanket appeal.

That afternoon at Panhandle, understanding nothing of all of the controversy about the participation of whites, I assumed that we were needed simply because the Movement wanted to build an internal brotherhood. I decided to go South as soon as I'd scanned the brochure. I believe my motivation had less to do with my dating Annette than with something else: I was a Young Democrat, foolish enough to believe Party leaders who said that citizenship, not race or class, was the subject matter of American politics.

I knew of course, that there was small chance that I might get killed, but the prospect wasn't particularly dispelling: as an ROTC student, I also knew that there was a war in Vietnam. In those days, a lot of young men grew up thinking that the risk of death in the name of a cause was an inevitable passage to adulthood.

Nor did I think—even for a minute—that I was going into an environment that was in any way foreign to me. Texas was segregated; Oklahoma, too. Colleges and some high schools had been integrated, but Annette Owens and I saw each other secretly because appearing together in public wasn't safe.

The brochure set forth terms for work with several organizations. All of them promised to lodge their volunteers with black Movement families, but SNCC planned to select only a handful of volunteers, and could not pay stipends. SCLC wanted to recruit hundreds of summer workers, and offered a stipend of $12.50 a week. The money that SCLC (called "SLICK" by SNCC rivals) promised wasn't much, but I had no resources and expected none. Immediately I wrote a letter asking the group to count me into its summer program, called SCOPE, for Summer Community Organizing and Political Education. SCOPE's purpose was to organize people to demand the vote, and in order to help overcome the literacy tests that were imposed on prospective voters, to teach the basic lessons of civics texts.

I didn't know it, and I'm not sure that anybody was aware, but SCOPE represented a dramatic shift in the character of the civil rights movement. Always before, at least until the passage of the Civil Rights Act of 1964, the Movement had in many ways pleaded—though sometimes in militant ways—for whites to accept blacks. The shift towards political organizing meant that the Movement would henceforth demand not a seat next to whites in a diner, but the seat on which the whites were sitting: it was a struggle to take from whites the seats of power and patronage. Since white people already occupied almost all of the political positions in the South, and there was little room for expansion—a city can have only one mayor, a county, only one sheriff—the Movement was not asking for acceptance, tolerance, or love: it was demanding power.

When a movement sets out to capture political power, it soon finds that power and prosperity are links in the same chain, and if people vote on paper, at the ballot box, people also cast votes at the cash register with every purchase that they make. If people are to be represented politically, they will soon demand that their economic ballots buy representation, too. Boycotts and a struggle for black employment across the economic spectrum were a natural extension of the logic of political enfranchisement. After the enactment of the Civil Rights Act of 1964, the Movement wasn't asking anybody for acceptance: it became a movement for power and economic position.

My decision to go South was made without consultations with anybody, and without the consent of my parents. I soon went to inform them. They had recently moved to Dumas, a refining, wheat-and-sugar beet town at the northern tip of Texas. I dreaded the business of explaining myself to them, because though few adolescents truly know their parents—knowing would mean admitting a sameness—I knew that they would be opposed.

It wasn't that they were racists. Things weren't as simple as that. My mother is a folkloric character, a Dust Bowl Okie who has never left her upbringing. Profoundly instinctive and sly, she's a shrewd player at dominos and bridge. Her ideology is that of the First (Southern) Baptist Church, no matter what the town. First Baptist Churches in the South are composed of farmers, foremen, and small businessmen; the economically marginal usually belong to more passionate congregations. First Baptists, in those days before the abortion debate, were sure that God was in His heaven and that all was right with the world. Therefore, they rarely railed against anything but alcohol. Her attitude towards me going South, I knew, would have nothing to do with talk of politics or power. She would object, I was sure, because in the near-perfect world in which we lived, white people weren't supposed to take up residence on the black side of town.

Dad, I figured, would be a much tougher case because of his testy temperament. He had come from the same dusty red plains that had produced my mother. His father had been a ne'er-do-well printer and sometime publisher of weeklies, and Dad faced no better prospects until he'd become a flyboy officer during World War II. He'd come away from the War with enough savings to buy into a prospering small-town Texas newspaper, and our lives since had been a series of shifts to acquire new pinches of capital. In high school, when I had dated Angela Calzada, a Mexican-American, he'd been upset, not because she was bronze-skinned, but because I was hanging out with the daughter of a gas station manager. He thought that the Reavis name had come a long way up from the Dust

Bowl, and worried—ensuing years have shown that he worried with some justification—that I would carry it back to poverty.

The Dumas place where my parents lived was a typical split-level tract house of the sixties: central air conditioning, sheetrock walls, two-car garage, a cedar fence surrounding the backyard. Its kitchen sat on the back side of the upper level, facing over a counter into the living room. One night after supper, sitting at the bar, I announced what I intended to do.

My father called me into the living room, while my mother watched from the kitchen sink. Dad sat on a couch; I sat in an armchair facing him. His initial approach was one of indirect reasoning. The demonstrations of the Negroes, he said, were flawed on two scores. Many of their actions were illegal, and breaking the law wasn't justified so long as the legislative process was open, even if only to whites. The demonstrators also demanded "Freedom Now!" but immediate change was an infantile idea. History didn't work that way, he declared.

"What do you want the Negroes to do, wait another hundred years?" I asked him.

His grimace said that I was being impudent.

He grappled for words, exasperated.

My mother broke in, still drying dishes.

"I know what it is, Dick J.," she intoned. "At Panhandle, do you have a Negro girlfriend? Is that what it is?"

Because I knew her opinions, I lied.

"But doggone it," Dad sputtered. "Don't you see what they plan to do with you? The only reason that this Dr. King wants you down there is so that you'll get killed, like those three boys in Mississippi."

I shrugged.

"Don't you see," he continued. "If white kids die, then this Dr. King will get more publicity."

He had hit a nail on the head, and I couldn't get around it by lying. I considered the point.

"Dad," I said after awhile, "if we live in a country where nobody pays attention when Negroes die, then I guess that's the way it has to be. Somebody has to pay the price."

He didn't act as if I'd said anything noble, and I suppose that he was right: nobility is a characteristic of the mature, who have conflicting motives for everything. Logical consistency, on the other hand, is the ideal of academics and college students, whose best role is to demand that the rest of us be rational.

Mother came in from the kitchen and sat down beside him. Then Dad *really* explained.

He had bought two quarreling and unprofitable newspapers in Dumas, both of them badly in the red, and was in the process of merging them. One had been a free circulation or "throwaway," the other a five-day-a-week daily with little circulation.

Within weeks, a new competitor sprang up from the ranks of those who had formerly produced the "throwaway." This crimped Dad's plans, and at the moment that I came home to make my announcement, he was struggling for his business life.

To establish the combined newspaper, he needed an expanded circulation, and I was the key to that: in high school I'd sold subscriptions and managed newsstand distribution in two different towns. Dad wanted me to do the same during the summer in Dumas. If his new newspaper failed, the family failed, and the family included not only the three of us, but my elementary-age brothers as well. A part of the family's future was in my hands. I couldn't turn my back, he said.

Not for minute did I consider his plea. I didn't know enough to imagine the import of what he was saying. I didn't know how a mortgage works—or that our house was mortgaged—and it didn't worry me that in order to make the newspaper deal, Dad had borrowed money. As far as I was concerned, my parents were relatively rich and secure white folks, putting up the usual resistance to reform. My attitude was entirely just and even sagacious from the point of view of the world into which I was entering, and indeed, just as I expected, my parents prospered without my help. But from the point of view of the world that I was leaving, I had repudiated my debt to my kinship group.

By the time that the discussion ended, I knew better than to ask permission to take my car South; I didn't pay for insuring it, and couldn't pay. A few days later, my parents drove me to board a train for Atlanta. As the train pulled in, Dad handed me a twenty-dollar bill. I didn't know how to respond. It was as if he was for me and against me at the same time.

Chapter 2

I read in the paper,
just the other day,
Said the Freedom Fighters,
are on their way.
They're coming by bus,
and airplane, too.
And they'll even walk,
if you ask them to.
—Freedom Song

IN ATLANTA I HIRED A taxi for the first time in my life to take me from the train station to SCLC's offices on Auburn Avenue, the main street of the city's vast ghetto. The city was the largest I'd ever seen and the streets that the taxi coursed seemed to me a jumble. My Dad, I reflected, had probably felt the same mix of fascination and scorn when, in his flyboy days, he for the first time saw the world beyond the Plains.

A receptionist at SCLC's headquarters sent me to wait in a hallway. Meeting rooms were located along its course, and pretty soon a young man in his mid twenties came out of one of the rooms, dressed in carpenter's jeans and a blue chambray shirt, a version of the "Freedom Suit" that "Freedom Fighters" had originally adopted as a disguise. "So, doc, do you want to make yourself useful right now?" he asked, without any introduction or chitchat.

I was of course puzzled that he called me "doc," and soon would find it odd that every male involved in the Movement was "doc" or "doctor" whenever a colleague was addressing him. There may have been a reason for the nickname, though perhaps none of us knew what it was. Only a few SCLC bigwigs knew that some months earlier, the FBI had mailed Dr. King an audio tape, made by one of its bugging devices, in which he allegedly referred to liaisons with lovers as meetings "with a doctor." Among the ways of dealing with the FBI's blackmail threats would have been to confuse any future interpreters by making "doctor" the code name for dozens of people with whom King might have other reasons to meet. But I cannot know if things really happened that way, because SCLC staffers had always called Dr. King "Doc," and maybe the nickname had spread well before my time.

The young man in the Freedom Suit took me to a first-floor mailing room, where he told me to carry several boxes to trash containers in the alleyway. In the alley, I examined the contents of one. It was filled with copies of *The Crusader*, a periodical published by Robert Williams in Havana. Williams, who would later become a legendary figure in what would be called the black liberation movement, had been an official in a North Carolina chapter of the NAACP when racist goons threatened him. He and several others had armed themselves for self-defense, and had wound up facing felony charges. Rather than submit to trial, Williams had made his way to Cuba, from which he broadcast a weekly short-wave program called "Radio Free Dixie." I'd never heard of Williams or his cause, and the pages I leafed were provoking. They talked about an America in flames; one illustrated note explained how the components of air conditioners could be used to make bombs. Obviously, *The Crusader* was not the sort of publication that a non-violent group like SCLC wanted to circulate. But I slipped a copy of it into my duffel bag because I was intrigued by what we would today call its stand-up attitude.

As soon as I finished the dumping job, another came my way. The young man in the Freedom Suit, whose name was Stoney Cooks, had no driver's license. He said that the police in Florida or Georgia had suspended his license after arresting him on trumped-up charges. So he put me to work as his driver.

Our rounds in an old clunker ended at the SCOPE House, a white, two-story, Craftsman-style home where Dr. King had formerly lived. The SCOPE House was a "Movement house," the kind of place where organizers both lived and worked. Its first floor was crowded with desks and bookshelves and mimeograph machines. It also housed a big kitchen, from which meals were served. The second floor—I never saw it—was reserved for females. Males slept in the basement, where I dropped my duffel bag on an empty bunk.

The house was an indoor camp for two kinds of people: field and office staff. The field staffers, all males, were brought into Atlanta from small towns across the South only when they had business to do at the headquarters office. None of those on hand when I arrived were white.

The office staff may have included a white or two, but no males: Cooke, for example, was a field staffer, on temporary duty in the city. On the status scale of the Movement, field staffers were king: some of them had been brought to Atlanta from jails.

When I returned to the office floor, I witnessed a scene with a portent that I couldn't fathom. A half dozen whites, both male and female, had come in from the broad porch on the home's front side. They were standing in front of a desk where a secretary worked. The men were dressed in jeans and loose shirts. The women wore blousy one-piece dresses, which, like the men's garb, had never seen an iron. Both sexes were shod in sandals or tennis shoes. One of the men had a short beard, and all of the women had straight, flowing hair, not in keeping with the teased-and-sprayed style of the age. The word "hippie" had not yet been coined and would have been inappropriate, anyway. These kids looked like beatniks.

I didn't look anything like them. I was burr-headed and clean-shaven, and though I too wore jeans, my shirts were starched and pressed and impeccably white. I was the picture of Southern rural conservatism, they, of a rebellion whose features were as puzzling to me as their style of dress.

They were wrangling with the secretary. One of the guys was saying that yes, the group wanted to join the SCOPE project, but that it refused to participate if loyalty oaths were being required. The secretary was explaining that the matter of the oaths was being reconsidered, that no decision had been made. The discussion went on for a few minutes, and then the white kids turned, went out onto the porch and disappeared into the street. I couldn't imagine why they'd objected so much. Dr. King's movement had been accused of Communist infiltration, and though my opinions about Communism were far from formed, I believed that the Movement had no choice but to avoid appearances of impropriety.

When supper came, everyone in the SCOPE house was handed a plate and, because there was no dining room, I went to the back yard, where people were leaning about, eating as best they could. After the plates were returned to the kitchen, people returned to the yard and formed a circle. Somebody had a guitar. I walked up to the circle, but somebody waved me away. "Look, we'd prefer if you didn't join us until you've had a little time in the field," one of the men told me. Embarrassed, I went indoors. As I lay in my bunk, listening the others clap and sing their "Freedom Songs," I paged through *The Crusader*, trying to match the gentle scene outdoors to the rhetoric from Williams' pen. After deciding that I couldn't figure that out, I leafed through liberal and social democratic tracts about the Movement, which were lying about everywhere. None of them made much sense to me; I couldn't figure out what their message was. The main thing that I understood was that I was now in a place that was far from the clearly laid-out grids of the Plains.

Over the next couple of days, while the staffers prepared for the conference that would launch SCOPE, I worked as a driver and, one afternoon, as a canvasser in the state senate campaign of SNCC spokesman Julian Bond. A few months later Bond would be denied his seat in the Georgia legislature because he opposed the Vietnam War. But I knew nothing about his anti-war pronouncements, and they weren't mentioned on the flyers that we took from door to door in the ghetto. Had I known, I might have balked.

The SCOPE conference was to open with a speech by Dr. King. At the last minute, the location of the conference was changed from the auditorium of one black Atlanta university to the gymnasium of another, Morris Brown College. With a poorly-educated, terribly young black Southerner who claimed to be a field staffer, I was assigned to the parking lot of the first auditorium. Our job was to direct drivers to Morris Brown. My partner wore the formal version of the Freedom Suit: a dark tie, starched overalls, and a white dress shirt. Like most veterans of the field, he also wore a broad-brimmed straw hat. Beneath it were a pair of sunglasses that he perched mid-way down the bridge of his nose, tilting his head forward to look over them—as if they were made to be obstacles instead of aids. The field staffers were always short of money, it seemed, and were constantly bumming cigarettes from me. As the Sunglasses Kid and I stood, smoking and sweating beneath a midmorning sun, I remarked that I'd rather be at Morris Brown, listening to Dr. King.

He almost spit out contempt.

"Shit," he said, "they ain't going to be doing nothing. Nothing but talking about where the Movement is going. If anybody knew that, then it wouldn't be no Movement!"

It was as if he regarded speeches and conferences as something that we did for show, or from pretension, or because the Movement was confused.

About noon we eased over to Morris Brown and entered the gym. The SCOPE kick-off was running late. Dr. King hadn't appeared and other speakers were killing time, like musicians in an opening band. I sat down in a folding chair and made a quick study of those who had filled the venue.

The number seemed greater to me, but sociologists who were on hand later said that only some 300 people turned out for SCOPE. Most of them, about 270, were white college students. They looked like the Beatnik Kids that I had seen at the SCOPE house disputing the loyalty oaths. Half or more of their number were female. There were also a few dozen older white men, professors, professionals, and experts of various kinds, who were in Atlanta to study the process and provide advice. The scattering of black students weren't unkempt, like the whites; they wore Freedom garb or clothing of the stiff, shiny style of the times. Two dozen men in Freedom Suits, field staffers, stood in the grandstands or moved in and out of the gym, ignoring the speeches. Two dozen other black males in inexpensive business suits were seated at the front of the place, beneath the podium. These were ministers from small towns, on hand to voice support, or to ask for aid, or merely to admire Dr. King's speechifying.

I didn't see anybody who looked like me.

King's phalanx came in from the back of the gymnasium, its members nearly pushing him along. He was not a striking figure, as I'd expected. Instead, wearing a narrow-brimmed straw hat and an ordinary brown suit, surrounded by men of a similar age and extraction, he looked like one pudgy guy among many. If any trait distinguished him, I thought, it was that he was shorter than I'd supposed. But when he began to speak, he carried me and his audience away. The nation had not known oratory like his in more than a generation before he came, and no one has spoken with such eloquence since his death.

What Dr. King had to say, I don't recall, and I doubt if I understood. It probably went over my head.

After he'd spoken for a half hour and made his exit, everyone went out and formed a line for a cafeteria lunch. As we were standing in the line, two men in field staffer garb came over and began passing out small flyers. They began their distribution at the end of the line. I was in the middle. Before they reached me, other men in Freedom Suits appeared, shouting angry words at the two leafletters, who vanished in a second's time. The interlopers were SNCC staffers, somebody said. Their leaflets complained that SCLC hadn't declared opposition to the war in Vietnam. The field staffers passed down the line, collecting the offending flyers, lest they be circulated by sympathetic SCOPEs.

Inside the cafeteria, I took a chair at a table where four or five young white students sat. They didn't look like Beatniks. They looked like surfers. They were Californians, and at least one of them, at seventeen, was two years younger than me. They were mulling over King's speech, which they hadn't liked. King hadn't mentioned Vietnam; he was holding out, they said.

The Californians were wearing celluloid pins on their shirts. The pins carried a logo that, to me, looked like a chicken track inside of circle. I asked what the pins represented, and one of them told me, a bit sneeringly, that the "chicken track" was the universal sign for nuclear disarmament. "It's come to be worn as a protest against the war in Vietnam," he explained. Then he described for me the California crew's involvement in SANE, an anti-nuclear weapons group. The Californians also told me that Movement sympathizers in California had organized a support group to send them to Dixie as SCOPES.

"How can you guys do all of this?" I asked in complete innocence. "What do your parents say?"

"I'll tell you what," the seventeen-year-old said to me. "Mine were practically pushing me to come down here."

I was jolted into the silence of awe.

During that week, we SCOPES were quartered in a dormitory with people from the field staff. We spent the daytimes listening to speeches about the Movement's history and aims, and the evenings in spontaneous bull sessions and song fests. Among those who spoke to us in the gym was the left-wing radical Bayard Rustin, and if my memory serves me right, Michael Harrington, a nominal socialist and author of *The Other America*, a book that had upset the nation by exposing the existence of poverty among both blacks and whites. But most of what the experts and academics said went by me, couched as it was in a social democratic vernacular that I didn't understand.

I comprehended more of what was said in the bull sessions. Typically, a group would gather in someone's room and field staffers would drop by to give their perspective on whatever was being said. During the discussions that I witnessed, I noticed that the field staffers were, as a group, stoic and reserved, but I couldn't tell if it was their experience or their mostly-Southern origins that gave them that attitude. The real radicals in the dorms were the African Americans from Up North. "What this Movement is about," I recall one of them screaming, "is black supremacy. We want 400 years of black supremacy! That's the only thing that will remedy 400 years of white tyranny!" When things like this were said, the field staffers usually muttered things like "doctor, you should calm down."

The field staffers were expressing their sincere opinions, I believe, not merely supervising. In one discussion, someone advocated revolution and socialism. A staffer who was in the room prefaced his commentary by repeating "Now, I ain't no Communist"—he said that several times— but he voiced support for most of the points that the revolutionary had made. I was shocked, more than I had been by the spokesman for black supremacy, because I wasn't used to being around what were called Comsymps, or communist sympathizers.

On the second or third day of the conference, the people in some of the dorm rooms found that their belongings had been rifled, and that valuables were gone. The gossip among SCOPEs was that a couple of field staffers had made a heist; they had keys to the dorm, it was said. But the field staffers laid the blame at the feet of hoodlums from a rough neighborhood near the campus. Nobody ever knew who the thieves were, but the thieves had to know that they were practically stealing from a priesthood, or a church, dedicated to the welfare of the poor. With that incident, we encountered, as an obstacle and a threat, the burgeoning and treacherous power of the underclass. But nobody discussed the implications. Like good urbanites, the volunteers merely shrugged off the thefts.

When bull sessions adjourned in the rooms of strangers, they resumed in the room where one slept. There were two couch-like beds in the room to which I was assigned, but since things were crowded, I and two or three extra people slept on blankets on the floor. My roommates were an education to me, because I had never known anyone like any of them. One was a Jewish student from Philadelphia, a member of the pacifist Fellowship of Reconciliation, who on moral grounds wouldn't kill a cockroach that I spotted on our windowsill. Another was a black student from Atlanta who hadn't decided whether or not he'd stay with SCOPE. Its program was competing for his attention with the chance to take opera lessons in New York. I couldn't understand the motivations of either of them.

As I ran into people and ideas that were foreign and often displeasing, a thought began to grow in my mind. It's the same thought that, in the corporate world, is praised as "team play," and in politics, is condemned as and practiced as partisanship. It was: whoever is in the Movement is all right. I took that idea to heart, for reasons that I thought were altruistic. But the truth is, I had to think in terms of team play. Otherwise, I'd have been alone—for, white and Southern and barely liberal, I wasn't like anybody else there.

I had special difficulty with the seventeen-year-old Californian who camped in our room, one of the group that I'd met in the cafeteria. One night he told me that he'd be going out of the dorm, to attend a party.

"There are some girls in from a youth group in Selma, and I hear that they're just looking for white boys," he said, inviting me along.

"But you can't do that," I cautioned.

"Why not?"

"Didn't you hear Reverend Young's speech?" I asked.

Earlier in the day, the Reverend Andrew Young, an SCLC spokesman—later to be Andy Young, President Carter's representative to the UN—had addressed the whole gymnasium on the subject of sex. SCOPEs would be going into communities where romance and jealousies already existed, and we weren't to add to those divisions, he'd said. In particular, whites and blacks were not to cross the sexual color lines. "We don't want more 'Freedom Babies'," he exclaimed; the field staffers applauded and cheered. "Freedom Babies," I'd learned, were the offspring of trysts between Movement visitors and locals. I gulped as I listened to all of this—and decided to follow orders.

"Ah, but he didn't mean any of that," my California colleague was telling me. "You should have seen *him* twisting with the white girls at the party where I was last night."

I gulped again, and let the Californian go on his way.

Hours later, he shook me by the shoulder as I slept on the floor.

"I got me one!" he exclaimed in a whisper.

"You did what?" I said, trying to roust my senses.

"I got me a little black baby!"

"What?" I asked, not believing the words that I was hearing.

"You know, I took one of those girls from Selma off into a bedroom, and you know, we did it."

I rolled over, my head to the floor, trying to deny what I was hearing and reminding myself—it was my first real strain—that "if he's in the Movement, he's all right."

I'd been at the conference only a day or two before I began seeking others of my kind. My concerns were not narrowly personal, though they were that as well. I correctly assumed that the participation of Northern volunteers in the life of the South would be episodic. The future of the region, I believed, would fall upon the shoulders of its natives, black and white. A new black leadership was in evidence across the Movement—future officeholders, I figured—but whites weren't to be seen. It didn't seem possible that whites could be eliminated from the region's political life, and I presumed that Movement blacks, once in office, wouldn't deal with whites who came from segregated country club and fraternity backgrounds. I wanted to meet the Southern whites with whom, I presumed, I'd someday share political schemes.

The sociologists who tracked the project would calculate that there were from fifteen to thirty Southern whites in the project. But I didn't find any, and the field staffers couldn't direct me to any of them; maybe those "Southerners" were Yankees from colleges in the South. There was a Georgia white on the field staff, I was told, but nobody seemed to know where he might be found. The field staffers spoke of him as of an eminence. They were friendly to my queries and usually, after mentioning the Georgian, they'd think a minute, smile and say something like, "You'd probably like to meet up with ole 'Arkansas'." Then they'd glance around the gymnasium as if he might appear at any time. But he wasn't there. They'd spend a few minutes telling me about a figure who had come to the Selma march, gotten his nose broken by the police, stayed on, and acquired a reputation as a fearless and undisciplined firebrand, a guerrilla. "You might try looking for him in Greensboro or Demopolis, he's been in those towns," some advised. "But he's not really with SCLC," they'd add with chuckle, as if talking about a slightly crazy man. They'd grin at one another and chortle, "If that doesn't work, try SNCC. That's where he *really* belongs!"

African-American interfaith and secular organizations across the South had affiliated with SCLC, and many of these groups sent representatives to speak at the conference, hoping to enlist SCOPE volunteers for work in their towns. When the staffers told me that the figure called "Arkansas" had been in Demopolis, the name stuck with me, though I'd never heard of the place. Soon I noticed that Demopolis was mentioned from the podium every day. After the Selma march staffers had spread out across Alabama to help local groups organize. The effort had sparked several little Selmas, especially at Camden—where "Arkansas" had been beaten by policemen—and at Demopolis, a town of 7,000, in a county called Marengo, located about midway between Selma and Meridian, Mississippi. The Camden conflict had apparently waned, but Demopolis was smoldering still.

Ralph Abernathy, Dr. King's second-in-command, spoke about Marengo, from which he hailed. Staffers cited it as a test of the organization's strength and changing base of support. The local groups that affiliated with SCLC were usually dominated by preachers, teachers, and small businessmen, people of the educated classes—people with a relatively conservative outlook. But in Demopolis the clergy and other "respectables" had deferred to the strength of a poorly-educated but handsome leader in his twenties, a cement finisher named Henry Haskins Jr. He also spoke to the SCOPE conference. On the podium, he cut a figure: tall, shining, ebony with chiseled, muscular features, he was an Adonis with a flat top. When he spoke to us, he wore not a business suit, but a striped short sleeved shirt, open at the collar, the Sunday go-to-meeting clothes of the working class. His voice was as sonorous as Abernathy's, and his style, snappy and hip, not heavy-laden with "preacher jive." He appealed to the left-wing bias of his crowd with an anecdote:

"When I was leading that march to downtown Demopolis," he'd said, "there were white folks standing on the sidewalks, yelling, 'Communist! Communist! Go back to Russia!' So I stopped the march," he said, thrusting his arms above his head, to show the gesture he'd used. "I stopped the march and I turned around and I looked at those white folks and I said, 'Communist? Communist? Why six months ago, I was only a nigger. I must be moving up in the world!'"

The gymnasium roared with laughter.

Half or more of SCLC's staffers had been in Demopolis in April and early May. Dr. King had stopped in for a speech. Haskins and the field staff had organized the big march downtown, and some 600 people had been arrested. Their number had filled both the municipal and county jails. The Movement had launched a boycott of the black schools, and had called for a boycott of the business district, where blacks were hired only as menials, never as cashiers or clerks. Television crews filmed much of the action, but Demopolis had not become as notorious as Selma, perhaps because the nation's viewers hadn't yet absorbed the Selma events.

SCLC's usual strategy was to precipitate a crisis, as in Birmingham and Albany, then set up a committee, usually led by Andrew Young, to negotiate a reduction in tensions in exchange for promises of amnesty, jobs, integration and public improvements. But in Demopolis SCLC hadn't been able to win at the bargaining table. They'd been able to wrest a few factory jobs from the white civic leaders, but retail jobs, for example, were still being denied to blacks. Things were at an inconclusive and doubtful stage.

Marengo County was also mentioned by the speakers because it was a part of the Black Belt, an area of a dozen counties in which African-Americans were a majority, or nearly so. Though the 1960 Census showed that Marengo, with a population of some 17,000, was nearly 70 percent black, flight to the north had begun. Families were giving high school seniors one-way bus tickets to Detroit as graduation gifts. In 1965, SCLC's estimates said, the population was only about half black. But even at that, blacks accounted for enough of the total population to give them electoral clout, if and when literacy requirements for voting could be overwhelmed. Forty percent of Marengo's black population was functionally illiterate. Organizing them to register and vote didn't promise to be easy.

SCOPE had plans to operate in the Carolinas, Florida, Georgia, Virginia and Alabama. Alabama's Governor was George Wallace, the leading segregationist of the day. The state was the toughest on the SCLC list, and I thought it would be an honor to face whatever it might send my way. So I approached Haskins. I asked if "Arkansas" was there. Unlike the staffers, Henry didn't chortle or smile when he talked about the man; it was as if he held him in high regard. "He's over in Mississippi right now, helping out SNCC," he said. "But you should come on down. He'll be back and you can meet him then." I applied for assignment to Demopolis and when the conference ended, found myself headed there.

Chapter 3

OUR SATURDAY TRIP TO ALABAMA occurred in a world that no longer exists. Three vehicles were in our convoy, two sedans and a station wagon. We left in midafternoon, with a four-to-five-hour drive ahead. In Georgia, precautions were deemed unnecessary, but as we crossed into Alabama about nightfall, the driver of the station wagon in which three other white SCOPEs and I were riding, explained a policy about "integrated cars." The term needed some explanation.

In the South from Reconstruction until 1964—and in some places, afterwards—all social arrangements reflected a caste system based on color. Under penalty of law, whites and blacks used separate bathrooms, eateries, water fountains, etc. Blacks weren't permitted to try on clothing at department stores, nor to be on the streets of white residential districts after sundown. The regime was so thorough that the Southern Building Code called for racially separate waiting rooms in bus stations, hospital offices, and the like. The Civil Rights Act of 1964 supposedly removed these barriers, but it couldn't always reach into behaviors governed by custom: blacks weren't customarily permitted to enter the front doors of white people's houses, for example, and no law could give them entry there.

By law blacks had been assigned to the back seats of buses, streetcars, and trains. Autos were also segregated, according to a fairly complex and entirely customary code. In those days, bucket seats were for sports cars. Bench seats were standard equipment on most passenger vehicles. A white and a black male could ride in the front seat of a vehicle, but if several males of different races were to be seated in the same vehicle, separation was expected, whites in front, blacks in back. White and black females were likewise required to separate, one race in the back seat, one in front. White males and black females could ride in the same seat—though whites regarded it as racy—but it was dangerous for black males and white females to ride in the same seat: Klansmen had killed Mrs. Liuzzo because she was riding in the front seat with a black male. Except for the case of chauffeurs—who were usually black and whose passengers, usually white, rode in the back seats—driving was presumed to be the station of superiority. If several whites were riding in a car with several blacks, a white was expected to be at the wheel: in segregationist eyes, anything else looked sleazy or low-down.

The driver of our station wagon was an SCLC staffer, the Reverend Samuel B. Wells, a square-shouldered, jet black man with deep-set eyes. He'd been a freight handler and apparently, only a part-time preacher until he had come into the Movement during the Albany campaign, years before. By 1965 he was of middle age, and had achieved a nearly executive status in SCLC; I don't think I ever saw him wearing anything but a dark business suit. He'd been assigned to supervise work in Demopolis.

Henry Haskins Jr. rode next to him. In the back seat were two white SCOPE females, and one male volunteer, also white. I'd taken the rearmost space, in the station wagon's luggage compartment. Any cop who glanced at our seating arrangement would have known in an instant that we weren't, for example, a chess team from Georgia Tech or Tulane. Wells instructed us SCOPEs to duck out of sight whenever we entered a town, spotted an oncoming vehicle, or were being followed.

Sometime after we crossed into Alabama, the other SCOPEs mentioned my regionality. They wanted to know what it felt like to be a white Southerner. At the time, the question was new to me, and—though I still don't have much to say—I wound up talking nonsense about okra and grits. Mine was a harmless answer and the three SCOPEs let it pass, but, I note—the onus of explanation was on me. Northerners believed, with justifications that seemed obvious, that their regional heritage was blessed. Almost nobody realized that beneath Southern segregation lay an oppression that was everywhere the same.

At Eutaw or Greensboro, the three SCOPEs got out on the parking lot of a housing project where Movement folk lived. One car was to follow us to Demopolis, the other stayed behind. Out of the follow-up car, carrying a black pasteboard guitar case, came Jimmy Collier, a yellow-brown staffer in his mid-twenties. Collier was SCLC's minstrel. Whenever Dr. King went on a tour, Collier would join him on stage, providing Freedom Songs. I remember him as having thick woolly curls, always in need of a haircut, except for once, when he was just back from a tour. When Collier was with King, he got a haircut, wore clean clothes and ate square meals.

His familiarity with Wells and Haskins told me that he'd been in Demopolis before, and since he sat down in the station wagon next to me, I figured that he was headed there again.

About 10:00 P.M. our two vehicles came into Demopolis and were promptly at Henry Jr.'s white, wooden-frame, two bedroom house, which stood only a few feet from the curb. Henry's house was on the north side of the street, two lots west of the corner of his block. Eastward across the corner was the complex that housed the black schools. Across the street from Henry's house was the Morning Star Baptist Church, the headquarters of Movement activity. A police car was waiting in the schools' parking lot. Another was waiting beside the church. Both of the cars were pointed west; their drivers knew what direction we'd be coming from.

The two cruisers moved into position, one in front of our station wagon, one behind the trailing car. We heard doors slam as four cops got out, two from each white cruiser. Three men approached us, two from behind, one from in front; one cop held back, standing beside his car door. The cops carried long metal flashlights, but they weren't shining their beams. Staring into the darkness, Henry recognized the face of one of them, a tall, strongly-built white male.

"It's Sergeant Johnson," he muttered.

There was a rustling in the car. Somebody groaned as if to say, "oh, no."

The two cops from behind us walked past the trailing car and gathered at the window of our back seat. The cop from the front, Sergeant Johnson, who turned out to be a man in his thirties, came to the driver's window.

"Good evening, Reverend Wells. I've got a warrant for your arrest," he said triumphantly.

"What's this?" the Reverend grumbled.

"Come on, get out of the car, we've got a warrant. It's from Georgia, for child support."

Wells cast a mournful look at Haskins. They exchanged some words whose upshot was that the charge wasn't fabricated; Wells apparently had a wife or ex-wife whose anger or impoverishment lay at bottom on the affair. I was a bit shocked, but mainly, I was afraid.

"Come on, we're going to jail," Sergeant Johnson told Wells, waving his flashlight impatiently.

Wells meekly opened the door and stood on the sidewalk, straightening his coat. Sergeant Johnson leaned into the open window, shining his light now. The two other cops pointed lights into Collier's window, which was closed.

"Now, just who have we got here?" Johnson asked, smirking at Haskins.

Haskins didn't answer. He turned his eyes away, gazing straight through the windshield.

Johnson motioned with his flashlight. The waiting cop came up. He was older, thin, bony, with graying hair. He stared over Johnson's shoulder.

"Chief Cooper, just who have we got here?" Johnson asked him.

Cooper poked his head inside.

"Well, now, there's Henry, we all know him," he drawled. "And let's see"—his eyes passed over me—"you're Jimmy Collier, aren't you?"

"Yeah, that's my name," Collier grunted.

"And Jimmy, whereabouts around here do you live?"

Collier cited a street address in one of the Northern states, Ohio or Illinois.

"But I asked you, where are you going to be staying here in Demopolis?" the Chief repeated.

"Chief Cooper, you know that the Supreme Court says that all I have to tell you is my name and permanent home address," Collier said, leaning back in the seat as if bracing himself for a blow.

"Now, Jimmy, the Supreme Court is in Washington and you're in Alabama," the Chief reasoned.

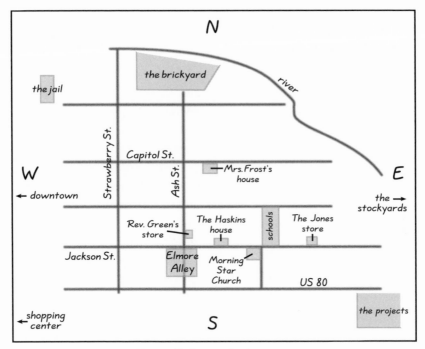

Demopolis from author's memory

Collier looked straight forward. He didn't say anything.

"Well, Jimmy aren't you going to tell me?" the Chief insisted.

"I've told you what I'm going to say," Collier said.

"Well, all right, you step out, too. You're both going to jail!" said the Chief.

Collier glanced over at me as he reached for the door handle.

"And who are you?" the Chief asked me.

I gave him my name.

"Boy, where are you from?" Sergeant Johnson boomed, as if he'd picked up on my twang.

"Texas," I told him.

"Texas!" he repeated, turning to the cops on the sidewalk.

"Texas, Texas," passed from mouth to mouth.

Collier was now outside of the car. Sergeant Johnson leaned back into the front window.

"Texas—boy, you ain't going to turn out like that 'Arkansas,' are you?"

The cops quaked with laughter. Then they handcuffed their prisoners and were gone.

Henry Jr.'s house sat on the south, or front end of a lot. On its north or back side stood "My Dear's house," the home of his mother, Mrs. Julia Haskins, "My Dear" being the customary title for one's mother. My Dear's wood-frame house was somewhat larger than Henry's place, but much older. Its roof seemed to sag and its outer walls were sheathed in tarpaper siding with a mock brick design. Perhaps fifteen yards of grassy area and a ten-foot concrete patio, leading up to My Dear's door, separated the two. Beside the patio stood a venerable tree—of which species, I do not know—that was the only sizable one on the lot.

Three SCOPEs had been passengers in the car that trailed our station wagon. All were female. I don't think that I chatted with them Saturday night, other than, perhaps, to pass on my account of the arrests. We did not talk at length because they were quickly ushered to My Dear's house. I was assigned for the night to Henry Jr.'s house, which, he informed me, had a bathroom, i.e., a room for bathing, but no fixtures. Rising several times during the night, I went outside to smoke a cigarette and urinate on the lawn. I was nervous and afraid, and fear was new to me.

In the morning breakfast was given to me by Henry's wife, a somewhat chubby woman about his age and the mother of an eighteen-month-old child. While I was eating, the female SCOPEs came in from My Dear's house, but before we could converse, My Dear was upon us.

She was a dark, very heavy woman, probably weighing 250 pounds. Her face was puffy and her eyes glowed with life, but she wasn't a bubbly kind. My Dear Haskins was a tyrant. Dressed in floppy Sunday wear, she climbed the two or three steps into Henry Jr.'s house with her youngest son, Johnny Ray, guiding or lifting her by a forearm, like a handler bringing a boxer into the ring.

Johnny Ray was a graduating senior whose basketball scholarship had been imperiled by the spring boycott at the schools. He was a tall lad, with a long but not angular face, and he was usually pleasant, unlike his mom and dad, whom he obeyed in an exemplary manner.

My Dear seated herself in an armchair on the west wall of Henry Jr.'s living room. Johnny Ray, wearing starched overalls with a white shirt and tie, stood behind her. He called upon us SCOPEs to gather before them. Standing, we faced My Dear in a semicircle, with our backs to the livingroom's east wall. Henry Jr. sat in the kitchen, talking to Atlanta by telephone about the arrests of Wells and Collier.

My Dear told us that our job over the summer would be to assist the Demopolis Youth Committee with a voter registration campaign. The president of the DYC, she told us, was her son, Johnny Ray, who of course would report on our behavior. She then asked us to introduce ourselves, telling us to mention our church affiliations when we did.

The first to respond was a slender woman whom I remember as fair-skinned and freckled, with very curly red hair. I'll call her Little Red. She told My Dear that she'd come into the Movement from a campus in California, where she'd participated in student protests and worked in a SNCC support committee.

"Yeah, but what's your religion?" Johnny Ray asked when she was done.

"Well, I guess I'd say that if I had anything that could be called religion, it would be communism," Little Red declared.

"Communism?" My Dear shrieked.

She looked around at the rest of us, and then turned her attention back to Little Red.

"Child, you'd better get you a religion of some kind. When you go to church this morning, you pay attention, now."

It was a maternal rebuke, delivered in good cheer.

Next came the introduction of Linda Brown, a fashionably-dressed, lithe, green-eyed native of Harlem. Linda had golden skin and shoulder-length, straight black hair; one of her parents was Jewish, and the other, African-American. Her father, she would later confide to me, had been a reporter at the *New York Times* until McCarthyism came. He had been a member of the Communist Party, and because of that, had been demoted to a copy editor's job.

Like most Manhattanites, Linda was socially-conscious and cagey: she always knew what to say. What she told My Dear about her background I can't recall, except that she didn't mention church. When Johnny Ray asked, she claimed that her religion was African Methodist Episcopal, or A.M.E.—an answer that was entirely safe, at least around the Haskins house.

Then I spoke. I didn't have to say that I was from the South. My accent made that clear; Texas was only a clarifier. My Dear and Johnny Ray were enchanted.

"Huh, you're a cracker boy, that's what," My Dear jibed.

I blushed.

"Maybe you'll be like that 'Arkansas!'" My Dear enthused. "Isn't that what Sergeant Johnson told you last night?" She and Johnny Ray cracked up in laughter.

I was embarrassed, for I was coming to see that "Arkansas" was, if nothing else, a figure that stood out from everyone.

"What religion are you?" Johnny Ray asked, mindful that his mother's instructions were followed.

"I'm Baptist," I said, though it was hardly true.

I was sweating it. I'd been raised a Baptist, but Southern Baptists— all of whom were white in those days—weren't exactly like their black counterparts. Church tradition required congregations to vote on the acceptance of converts and transfer members, and across the region, Southern Baptists were voting to keep blacks out of their flocks. A maternal uncle of mine had stood to vote against an African-American newcomer to his church and I'd been wary ever since. I hadn't been to church since high school.

I said that I was Baptist mainly because I was terrified by Andrew Young's Atlanta speech. He'd told us SCOPEs that not only were we to be sexually on guard, but also that we should also attend church each week. "And I want you to sit on the mourner's bench," he'd preached. Mourner's benches existed in some rural Southern Baptist churches. I knew what they were, and I wanted to stay away from them. They were pews at the front of the sanctuary where the unconverted and wayward were supposed to sit, so that they could catch the brunt of the sermons. I didn't want to again have to "accept Jesus Christ as my Lord and Savior," as the phrase went. To avoid the mourner's bench, even at the expense of the truth, I feigned respect for the faith.

"Oh, that's good. You're from the same religion as us," My Dear said, nodding with a smile.

The first lie that I'd told in Demopolis had worked.

Ruth Levin was last to speak. She was a very light-skinned young woman with rosy cheeks, somewhat husky of build, with shoulder-

Ruth Levin, center, and Jimmy Collier, left, in My Dear Haskins' yard

length, fine, light brown hair, a student from Vermont who probably typified SCOPE. I can't remember her wearing anything but a white blouse, Bermuda shorts and sandals, though she must have owned other attire. Whatever Ruth said to My Dear about her preparation for the Movement I don't recall, because I was already shrinking from the response that was implied by her surname.

"And what religion are you?" Johnny Ray asked. It was by now routine.

"I'm Jewish," Ruth said in a voice that was quiet and firm.

My Dear threw a glance to Johnny Ray, who straightened his frame and gestured excitedly.

"Jewish? Well, if that's what you are," he exclaimed, "then you ain't got no religion at all."

My Dear nodded and scowled in agreement and the gathering began to disperse.

After church at the Morning Star—none of us sat on the mourner's bench—everyone gathered for a big luncheon served on My Dear's patio. On their way home from church the various hosts who would open their homes to SCOPEs dropped by to share the food and to arrange for our arrivals later that day. When the formalities of getting-to-know-you were done, we SCOPEs huddled behind Henry Jr.'s house, to elect a leadership, as My Dear had instructed.

The meeting took ten minutes, but its first order of business wasn't leadership. Little Red, Linda and Ruth whispered, was claiming to be ill. She had decided that she'd be going home. She stood on the edge of our circle as the two told this to me, and I merely nodded. We agreed that it was best to say nothing immediately to My Dear, because we thought that, rather than apologizing, she'd take offense. Ruth and Linda said that they'd walk Red to the bus station the following morning, as if her departure had been a spur-of-the-moment affair.

One of the two proposed that I be the leader of the remaining group of three. "But why me?" I asked, feeling quite flattered. "Because you're the only guy," Ruth said, "and besides that, you're going to live with the Haskins."

It was a future whose dynamics, I suspect, they had already figured out.

The Morning Star church

My Dear's house was to quarter me. The house, as I incompletely recall it, used a door facing the patio as an entrance. One entered a small kitchen. To the right of the kitchen, two narrow, rectangular bedrooms stood end-to-end; Johnny Ray Haskins slept in one, his younger sister, Virginia, in the other. A door at the end of the kitchen opened to a tiny bathroom, and to its left, shielded from view of the kitchen by a sheet hanging on wires, was a curtained bedroom. Beyond it was another divider, on whose far side slept My Dear and her husband, Henry Haskins Sr. a thin, graying, and very taciturn man. Somewhere, on the far left side of the kitchen, a low archway opened to a tiny living room, stuffed with knick-knacks and framed family photos. The house was crowded before I got there.

One of the curtained spaces was reserved for Julia Mae Haskins, who was shortly due home from a segregated state college. That left nowhere for me to sleep, except in the room with Johnny Ray, whose double bed occupied almost all of its space. He accepted me without any reticence. But he soon noted my fakery. Each night before retiring, Johnny Ray kneeled beside the bed to pray. I kneeled with him, but never tried to speak to God.

Queasiness about sharing a bed with a male was, for me, the second wrinkle of the day. Earlier I'd been called on to use my accent, and the exercise was unnerving. One of the problems that the Movement had across the South was that when its partisans went to jail, the authorities sometimes refused to free them on bond. They usually did that by keeping bond hearings and bond amounts a secret. In the counties outlying Marengo several activists were behind bars, with officials refusing to tell black visitors—and telephone voices that lacked a cracker whine—whether or not bonds had been set, and if so, what the amounts were. Somebody, perhaps a SCLC supervisor who was passing through town, gave me a list of three or four people who were in jail in a couple of counties where the authorities were playing the secrecy game. He asked me to call for bond information, pretending to be a local white. He also gave me a quick geography lesson—I don't think I ever saw a map of Alabama—and I gave it a try.

"Say, ya'll have got a boy in jail over there that sometimes works for us, over here at our Marengo farm," I'd stammer. "It's getting to where my dad needs him to work on the place, and we'd like to know—how much will it take to get him out on bond?"

The scheme worked every time. But it scared the life out of me, too. I had no moral qualms about deceiving the local whites. If they wouldn't disclose public information, deceit was what they deserved. But I was afraid that sooner or later, they'd find out who I was, and would then inflict upon me the hatreds and punishments that are everywhere reserved for traitors.

The following morning Johnny Ray presided at the meeting of the Demopolis Youth Committee. Perhaps twenty-five middle and high school students showed up. Johnny Ray introduced us SCOPEs and asked me to explain our mission. We'd brought with us from Atlanta fliers describing the program. We proposed dividing into teams to deliver the fliers, four or five DYC youth accompanying each of us SCOPEs on our first canvass of the black side of town.

I learned almost nothing useful that day because within minutes after we split up, for the first time in life, I was beset by an obstacle that I couldn't ignore. Totally to my surprise, I became an object of sexual desire. I'd left My Dear's house with four or five others, one of them a petite young woman whom I'll call Bronze Baby Bardot, or Miss 3Bs, for short. She was alluring, even sexy—but only fourteen. She was forward, too, immediately attaching herself to me, hands, eyes, and arms. As the group of us worked our way east of Henry's house and circled down again, her flirtations grew more direct, and the others fell further behind and drifted off, leaving us alone. I was caught in a bind. I felt flattered and teased. On the other hand, I felt terror: the kind of relationship that she wanted to ignite was just what Andrew Young had forbidden. I assumed that I'd be banned from the Movement if I gave in. But if I spurned her, I'd be labeled a racist, blue-nose or snob. As we came near the house where she lived, she whispered that nobody was at home: why didn't we stop by? At her front porch, I peeled her away, awkwardly saying that I had chores to attend to.

I found myself in a similarly delicate situation the following morning. A male from DYC walked me to the apartment where "The Twins" lived with their mother. The Twins, with whom I'd spend the rest of the day—my guide having slunk off somewhere—were identical sixteen-year-olds with shining yellow skin, hazel eyes and straight hair, as long as Linda Brown's. Their father, they told me as we made our rounds, had been a white man who sold insurance policies to blacks, door-to-door. A couple of times as we went from street to street, we encountered other DYC canvassing teams, and by day's end, when I left them at their mother's door, I was already hearing talk that I'd "picked the prettiest girls in town." Ten days later, when SCLC sent a technician to record the proceedings at a Demopolis mass meeting, a young man I hardly knew raised the "prettiest girls" charge for all to hear. Fortunately, I'd blocked its development. After my day with the Twins, I refused to work with female locals anymore.

Despite these distractions, before the week was over I'd mapped in my mind the area that I'd come to know, not only as a grid of streets, but house by house. Demopolis was more wretched than I'd expected, and in places, its poverty rivaled even the back streets of northern Mexico.

Henry's house lay nearly in the middle of the ghetto, bounded by a river on the north and east, the color-line street, called Strawberry, on the west, and U.S. Highway 80 on the south. Henry Jr.'s front door opened onto one of two main arteries through the black side of Demopolis, Jackson Street, which ran east to a stockyards, and west into the white district. The other chief artery, as pedestrians walked it, was Ash Street, a north-south street that intersected Jackson on the western corner of Henry's block.

Living conditions weren't uniform, but the spread was narrow. Going east on Jackson from Henry, Jr.'s, one came first to the Morning Star Church, on the block's southeastern corner, or right-hand side, and then to the schools, on the opposite side of the next block east. On the eastern edge of the school property was a general store operated by the Jones family—probably the most prosperous black family in Demopolis—and, nearby, the offices of their construction firm.

The houses along Jackson were of two types, either Victorian or ranch-style, like those in tract subdivisions, but humbler yet. Nearly all were of wood, and nearly every one was painted white. None of them, I believe, could have been younger than twenty years old, and the most venerable among them had been built before the turn of the century. Unlike homes in the northern United States, none had a basement. Second stories were rare. I recall none in the Jackson area, and two that I spotted, north of there, were used as rooming houses. Not many houses had garages; cars were parked at streetside, there being few curbs. Jackson and a few cross streets were paved, but most of the ghetto was dusty on dry days, muddy during rains. At the southeast corner of the ghetto, about ten blocks east of Henry and half as many south, was a modern, red-brick, public housing development where more than two dozen families lived. Its director, a kindly white, once told me that when he introduced new residents to the features of their apartments, those who were coming from the countryside usually asked how to operate a commode.

The area to the west of Henry's was also lined with Victorian and middle-aged ranch-style homes, as far as Strawberry Street, the color line. On two or three streets, in blocks just east of Strawberry, an oddly interracial pattern had evolved. Blacks lived on one side of these blocks, north or south, and whites lived on the other. Late in the afternoons, they'd gaze at each other from their front porches, never crossing the pavements to exchange neighborly news. Those blocks were, I always thought, slices from divided Berlin: wary encampments, living cheek by jowl.

The ghetto was home to the town's lower middle class, but two pockets of it were poorer than that. "Elmore Alley," where Miss 3Bs lived, lay a stone's throw from Henry's, half-a-block west, towards Strawberry. The two streets in Elmore Alley were only a block long; their corners split the opposing blocks, rather than matching the intersecting line. Elmore was the remnant of a turn-of-the-century lumber camp. Its shotgun houses were of rough-hewn pine, a few of them painted a barnyard red, most of them, paintless and gray. Their sheet metal roofs were warped and rusting, their yard areas, gone to dust. Like the Victorian-era homes, they'd been built before Demopolis was electrified, and before plumbing, too. A single bulb hung from a wire in each of Elmore's two-room shacks. A pipe ran to every kitchen, but sanitary plumbing was unknown. An outhouse stood in every back yard.

Just north of Henry's house, on Ash Street, was a small grocery store that was legendary in the local movement. It belonged to and was operated by the Reverend Percy Green, pastor of the Eastern Star Baptist Church, a man who wore wire-framed glasses and always wore a white shirt. The Reverend Green was what the Movement called an "Uncle Tom," or he had been a few months earlier, anyway. When the downtown boycott had started in March, with permission from the mayor, the Reverend Green had made a radio broadcast aimed at the town's blacks. "My friends, whenever we bring political structure into the House

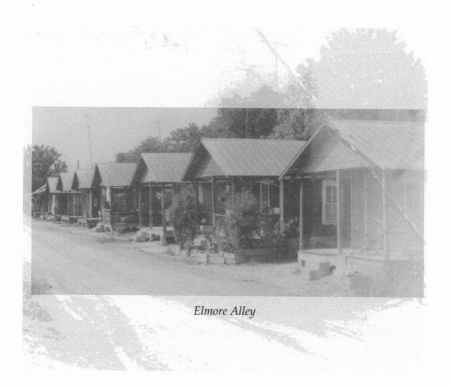

Elmore Alley

of God," he said, "or use it to teach youth and adults to group themselves together and stand in front of our business establishments and forbid our people to go in and buy what they desire, or if they go in and buy what they desire then have someone standing by to take the package from their arms and trample it upon the grounds, or to stain the House of God with such teachings that the Law of our land and those entrusted with upholding that law or laws with dignity will become suspicious. You have left teachings of Jesus Christ out of the church and Christ is not pleased with it," he preached.

His reference to the trampling of packages was accurate: high school kids had assaulted downtown shoppers as they made their way back into the ghetto. Their action probably wasn't popular, but when the Reverend Green, in the heat of a campaign that resulted in hundreds of arrests, had challenged the Movement's legitimacy over radio, he'd brought its force to bear on him. The Movement declared a boycott of his store, and several of the DYCers bragged to me that they'd "busted sacks" of people who'd continued to shop there. The Reverend Green also heard complaints from his congregation. Economically pressed, he'd capitulated. In exchange for the lifting of the boycott against his grocery, this "Uncle Tom" had declared support for the Movement, and two or three times during the summer, when we were hard-pressed for transportation, we stopped by the Reverend Green's store—and borrowed his car. His faith was no stronger than the pressures brought upon him, and from the date of his radio speech forward, the Movement had the stronger voice.

About three blocks west of Henry's and some six blocks north was a strip, not more than two blocks wide and two blocks long, of recent ranch-style and well-kept Victorian houses. Relatively prosperous families lived there: teachers, truck drivers, people with federal civil service jobs in Tuscaloosa, sixty miles away. Their dwellings were fully plumbed, and had garages and driveways. Window units air conditioned them in summer. In winter, no smoke rose there, as on the lumber camp streets. The new houses had wall and floor heaters fired by natural gas. This enclave was where SCLC got its foothold, by winning sponsorship from the Demopolis Civic Club, a time-honored, entirely black organization that existed to pay for, or ask for, maintenance of cemeteries and other segregated, but public facilities. Some of its members had been registered to vote even before Dr. King came to town.

If you walked north on Ash until you came to its end, you'd wind up in "The Brickyard." It lay along a bend formed by the Black Warrior Creek, as it split off from the Tombigbee River, on the white side of town. Trees and brush stood between the Brickyard's principal, dusty street and the creek. But its proximity to water was the only graceful feature of the place. Architecturally, the Brickyard was the same as Elmore Alley, but it was more forlorn. Some of its homes didn't have water lines. There was no glass—and may never have been—in most of its window frames. Screens lapped the openings in warm months, and in autumn, when temperatures dropped, residents tacked cardboard sheets in place, sealing out light as well as wind. The Brickyard was an area where, in simmering July, women sat on porches wearing only shorts and bras. Both they and their children went barefoot. The neighborhood's little girls made dolls by stuffing sections of rope into empty soft drink bottles; the resulting effigy, of course, had blonde "hair," which they stroked with combs. Two openly homosexual males lived together in a Brickyard shack; they were its only men. Brickyard fathers were in jail, on the lam, or simply forgotten and gone.

The Demopolis ghetto was a ward of the poor. It was not the America of two-car households, but the America of one-car and no-car households. It wasn't air-conditioned America, it was the America of fans and outhouses. The struggle its residents faced was, in their eyes, a struggle not so much for racial integration as for economic equality. They wanted to participate in the much-vaunted American dream, which was about having the money to live like the white folks lived, to go where the white folks went: it wasn't, as whites afterwards tended to think, a movement about fellowship with white folks.

SCLC, SCOPE and the local organizations faced slim odds in the effort to persuade the ghetto's residents that democracy was possible. Those who were ready to vote, besides the Civic Club types, were the youth, and they were too young. Working-age men were harried and pressed, and didn't have time for the procedures involved. Sooner or later they'd make time, I suspected, if only at the urging of the women and the kids; the mothers seemed more outspoken and brave. Much more difficult were the oldsters, who were numerous and scared, especially those men who worked in the countryside. We knew who they were as soon as we shook hands with them, because their palms were calloused: they still plowed behind mules. Some of the oldsters told us outright, "I ain't getting in that mess. Don't you come around here with that." Others feigned sympathy—and sadly, also feigned reading skills. They'd scan the lines of our fliers, while holding them upside-down. Most people over sixty couldn't read, though a good number had learned how to sign their names. In the Atlanta training sessions, we SCOPEs had been encouraged to review documents attesting to people's births, their military records and Social Security status. But with the old folks, it was of little use. In the main, they had spent their lives in agricultural pursuits. Many were therefore not eligible for Social Security, and if they were, they didn't know it. When asked where they were born, some of them would say things like, "On the Clark plantation." "Yeah, where's that?" we'd ask. "Well, they tell me that it's in Mississippi, but I was quite young when we left there, so really, I don't know." "Well, how old are you?" we'd follow. Pop would look at Mom or at Daughter Jane and quip, "Huh! They tell me that I'm about sixty-eight, maybe sixty-nine. Do I look that old to you?" The truth of the matter was that in their time nobody kept records of rural births, especially of plantation blacks. Since the old folks were obviously of voting age, we'd urge them to join the suffrage crusade even if they frankly admitted that they couldn't read. "But tell me, what is this voting business?" they'd inquire. They were unfamiliar with the fundamental ritual of American political life.

While I was still assessing the ghetto and its attitudes, my accent came back in demand. I was summoned to Henry Jr.'s to take a call from Hosea Williams in Atlanta. Hosea—everybody referred to him by his first name—was the fortyish King aide who was SCOPE's originator, its director, its unquestioned boss. I'd heard him speak at the conference, and perhaps, had shaken his hand, but he was the general in the army that I'd joined, and naturally I was apprehensive about dealing with him. He went directly to the point.

"They tell me that you've got a cracker accent and a driver's license," he said.

"Well, yessir, I guess that's true," I said.

"Well, listen up," he continued, "I need to know if you can do something for us. We've got an office staffer from the headquarters who's in jail over there in Mississippi."

"What's he in for?" I asked, merely to hold up my end of the talk.

"He stole a car from us," Williams said, without missing a beat. "Now, we need to know if you can take a bus over there, get him out, and bring the car to Demopolis," he said.

"Well, I guess I can," I said. But then—I'd later regret it—puzzlement got the best of me.

"If this guy stole a car from us, why do you want to get him out?" I asked.

There was a pause on the other end of the line.

Then Williams spoke, nearly in a rage.

"Well, maybe you don't know it yet, but we think there's already too many black folk in jail in Mississippi!"

"Yes, sir," I said. But I was still unconvinced.

Williams said that he'd call back if he needed me, to tell me where and how to make connections with a bondsman.

He never called.

I filed the incident in the back of my mind. Something suspicious was going on in the main office, it seemed. A thief was a thief, in my book—even a thief who was in the Movement, one of us. I didn't believe that Hosea would bail the man out for reasons of mere solidarity. But Williams, and Henry Jr., who spoke to him after I left the phone, may have come to a different conclusion, I realized. They may have decided that I was impertinent, or worse yet, still uncleansed of a cracker past.

I don't recall what happened to the Reverend Wells—maybe he was extradited to Georgia—but memory tells me that he was released after a time, and may have worked in Demopolis for several more weeks. Whatever he did, it didn't stick with me. It was Collier, released on bond late in the week, who got things moving faster than I'd imagined possible. His goal was to put together our first test of the Alabama literacy law.

The principle of the law was that having an educated electorate was fundamental to democracy. Rather than presuming a citizen's literacy, Alabama—and most Southern states—tested for it. In Marengo County, only school teachers and a few other blacks with college degrees could pass the tests. Whites nearly always did. The Movement's position was that literacy should not be a condition for political participation, and that the tests were administered according to racial standards. SCLC wanted the tests thrown out. But first, it had to prove that blacks were not allowed to take the test, or that, if they were allowed, they didn't pass it.

Voter registration tests were given, not every day, but only once or twice a month, on Tuesdays, as I recall. A registration day was coming up. Collier wanted us to convince people to go to Linden, the Marengo County seat, seventeen miles south of Demopolis, to apply for the tests. Under our supervision, prospective registrants were to form a line at the courthouse, which I recall as a building of Greek Revival style. (It burned to the ground in 1966.) The purpose of the exercise was to establish—for a Congressional hearing or Justice Department review—that Alabama's blacks were trying to exercise their citizenship rights, but being denied. We'd keep a roster of those who showed up, those who were examined, those who were turned away. Our canvassing efforts would be capped by a mass meeting at the Morning Star Church, on the upcoming Sunday or Monday. Collier went from door to door himself, knocking, announcing, cajoling. The rest of us did the same. More than

200 people attended the mass meeting; we knew that we were on our way. On Tuesday, dozens of cars ferried passengers to Linden.

I had a special role on that first day. I was to stay behind in Demopolis until the lines were formed. A local who owned a car waited with me. About noon a call came from Collier, saying that the hour had come. In Linden I walked past the line of waiting black registrants—it stretched outside and made a semicircle on the courthouse lawn—and went into the registrar's office, elbowing my way through waiting blacks at its door. At the registrar's counter, I explained my circumstances to a female clerk.

"Look," I said, in a hushed tone. "I've got my grandmother in the car. She's wanting to register. But you've got this line of niggers and she doesn't want to get in line with them."

The clerk nodded. She understood.

"What can I do?"

The clerk turned away from the counter, scanned the room, fixed her eyes on an older woman who was probably her boss, and then turned back.

"You see that door over to the left?" she said in a near-whisper.

I looked, and saw: to my right and behind the counter was a solid wooden door, probably leading into a hallway of some kind.

I nodded.

"Well, just bring her up there. Knock a few times, we'll know who it is and we'll let her in."

The trick had worked. I exited the building and conferred with Collier on the lawn. In Demopolis that night, he had me type an affidavit for the Justice Department, relating what I'd been told inside.

My special task finished, I hung around the courthouse. Collier gave me a list that he was compiling of the names of those in line. He flitted around, chatting, supervising, keeping an eye on things. I took up the list where he'd left off.

About an hour later—Collier must have been indoors—two deputies walked up to me. I braced myself, but they smiled.

"Say, they tell me you're from Texas," one of them said.

I nodded.

"Well, now, ain't that something!" he laughed.

"Well, at least they've figured out who I am," I said to myself.

I said nothing to him.

"Now tell me, I want to know if you'll help me with something," he continued.

I kept my silence.

"You see, we've got, or you folks, you've got this girl or young lady inside. She tells us her name is Linda Brown."

I nodded again.

The deputies closed in.

"We want to know, now, just what color is she? Is she white or Nigra?"

I grinned.

"You see," the deputy said, "she keeps walking from water fountain to water fountain, drinking from the colored fountain, then taking a drink from the fountain for whites. She keeps going back and forth like that."

I didn't say a word.

"Now, is she Nigra or white?"

It was clear that they intended to box-in Linda for an arrest. If she was white, they'd look foolish before a jury; whites could do as they pleased. But blacks—that was a different story. In Linda's case, the whole concept was ridiculous, though legally, in Alabama, she was black.

"I don't know what race she is," I lied. "You'll have to ask her."

"Huh, some boy from Texas you are," the deputy snorted.

Then both of them went away.

Linda wasn't arrested. Without information, Jim Crow couldn't make a case.

On a subsequent line-'em-up-at-the-courthouse day, a knot of us, perhaps fifteen in all, were waiting to be ferried back to Demopolis when someone suggested that we move across the street to the parking lot of the jail. Why we went there, I'm not sure. The sun was blazing and on the parking lot, there were no trees for shade. We formed a wide circle and sang Freedom Songs, maybe to dispel fear—carloads of thuggy whites were circling around—or simply to pass the time. Out of nowhere Miss 3Bs appeared to join the circle. She made a beeline for me, renewing her flirtations as if I'd never given offense. I swiveled and frowned, trying to drive her away. Then, without any warning, she fell to the pavement in a heap. I looked down at her, thinking that she was trying to trick me into taking her into my arms, and then skipped to the other side of the circle, irate. Women in the group lifted her up, and Ruth demanded that the police call an ambulance. When they refused, the women loaded her into a car that was Demopolis-bound. The next morning I learned that pregnancy had caused her fainting. But I didn't repent for having left her on the ground. Had I followed my more humane instincts, I'd have been rumored as the father of the baby that was on its way.

But the incident couldn't have won me any friends, and things were already going badly at the house. Suppers there were marvelous, with great portions of Southern cooking, well-prepared. But with meals there was talk, too. My Dear took the lead by denouncing racism in forms that I'd never imagined, and at first, found hard to accept. She'd say, for example, that "the crackers get their mail in the morning, but they don't bring it to us until afternoon." It was true, of course, and after thinking over charges like that, I came to see things more nearly her way.

It didn't stop there, however. She pressed me about my relationship with my parents. I said as little on the subject as possible, because there didn't seem to be much point. I didn't want to be rejected or accepted on the basis of their stand. Somehow she captured a caricature of my father, whom she began to index as "your cracker dad." She'd ask questions like, "what would your cracker dad say about that?" Repeatedly she brought up the subject and noticing my annoyance, sometimes referred to me as "cracker," too.

Things got unpleasant at times. One Saturday morning I noticed clothes piled on the patio and the family's old wringer-type machine, hooked-up and ready to go. I went inside, unpacked my duffel bag, and dumped my clothes with the others. Then I went back inside, and half an hour later, headed off again. Julia Mae, home from college, was standing at the washer. My Dear was sitting on a patio chair. As I passed, My Dear halted me.

"What do mean putting your clothes out there like that?" she barked.

I shrugged. "I don't know, I thought that that was what we were supposed to do," I said.

"What do you mean, 'supposed to do?'" she pressed. "Who ever told you to do that?"

I shrugged again, not understanding what was afoot.

"Listen, cracker boy," My Dear continued, "you're too used to having black folks do your washing for you, that's what."

It wasn't true. My mother didn't have a maid—but I said nothing.

"You pick up your clothes out of here and take them to the laundromat," she demanded.

I gathered up my things, asked about the location of the laundromat, and headed off, afraid. It was a block or two past the color line, on the white side of town. If I recall correctly, it was a part of the Lily White Laundry; a Demopolis business really had that name. On the way there, I met a DYC member, who advised me not to go. He took me to his house, where his mother was in the backyard, washing, as many Demopolis blacks did, by boiling clothing in a big cast iron pot over an open fire. For a couple of dollars, she agreed to do the job.

But I realized that I had made a mistake to assume that I was a member of the family. I should have asked if my clothes could be washed with the others. My lack of courtesy had become a racial incident.

That afternoon when I came back, a letter was waiting from me, from Annette, my girlfriend at college. She wrote that she'd begun dating someone of her own race and that she wished me the best. Reading her note I felt a letdown. I was now living in another world, one disjointed from the past. The Dear John only confirmed that.

Jimmy Collier wasn't wasting any time. As soon as we'd finished the first line-'em-up day, he'd thrown himself into SCLC's second project for Demopolis, the downtown boycott. Its object was to discourage people from shopping in Demopolis until its stores agreed to hire blacks as cashiers and clerks. Jimmy's first chore was to get approval from the Civic Club for the tactic he had in mind, which was illegal, according to state law. At his urging, the group's executive committee gathered on a lawn of a member's house to hear the case he'd make. I accompanied him to the session.

Collier planned a picket of a newly-built strip shopping center that lay near the color line. Arrests would come, Jimmy said, when pickets approached the stores. He thought it necessary to picket, partly because the action would spread word of the boycott into the rural areas. DYC and SCOPE would recruit the youth to man the picket lines and he'd supervise the action. SCLC would provide bail and a legal defense.

The leaders questioned only one point. They didn't want any whites to take part. Our presence on the picket lines, they said, would unnecessarily inflame local whites. Their objection meant that Ruth and I couldn't join the pickets.

The Civic Club leaders pointed out that the town's blacks had to shop somewhere, if only for groceries. Linden was only half the size of Demopolis, and by reputation was an even more racist town. They suggested that we encourage people to shop in Uniontown, an all-black settlement in Perry County, some twenty miles east. The next day, some of the locals took Collier and me to see the place.

It was a crossroads town where gasoline, groceries, and clothing were sold, but not much else. I was tempted, anyway. I had already decided to buy two items, a broad-brimmed straw hat, easily found, and a set of overalls, for my Freedom Suit. I wanted overalls like Jimmy and the other field staffers wore, whose external, backside label read, "Give Me LIBERTY," Liberty being a brand name. But I was too short or too small to be fitted. I had to settle for a different mark, one whose label showed a railroad roundhouse.

Like everybody else, before the summer was done, I was wearing a toothbrush on a key chain that I hung from a hole in the Freedom Suit overalls. The toothbrush demonstrated a willingness to go to jail, though as events soon showed, I wasn't quite ready. Adolescents try to define themselves by brand-name purchases, and I was no different from the rest.

My Freedom Suit got its trial the day after I bought it. A staffer whom I remember only as Jerry had come into town for the summer. He was an average-size young man in his mid twenties with a rounded mahogany face and a wisp of a mustache. Unlike the rest of us, he had a car of his own. But he couldn't drive it legally. He'd lost his license during a prison term in Georgia, his home state. He'd been in prison for six months or a year, on a felony charge—corrupting minors, or somesuch—arising out of a school boycott. Stories like his, of people who suffered great wrongs at the hands of the Southern judiciary, were common in Movement ranks—and I might note, our criminal records have never been expunged. As a convicted felon, Jerry probably faces restrictions today.

Jerry had been sent to Alabama to talk up the movement among people in the farm population, with upcoming federal agricultural hearings in mind. His territory included more than Marengo County. The day after Collier and I returned from Uniontown, Jerry wanted to make a visit to Greene County, across the Tombigbee. He asked me to drive.

About twenty miles into farm country we came to a spot where several family-sized army surplus tents stood in the middle of a fallow field, a squatter's camp. The tenant families that were living there had been thrown off their land because the women had tried to take the voter registration test, I believe. They were supporters of SNCC. Field staffer H. Rap Brown—later to become notorious as a "Black Power" chairman of SNCC—was on the grounds. When we pulled up, Jerry told me to stay outside of the tents unless he signaled me to enter. "I'm not sure they'll let you in," he advised.

My exclusion didn't perturb me much. It was becoming clear to me that I was in the Movement as a guest, at the pleasure of my hosts, for whatever purposes they might discern. In any case, I had no assignment to work in Greene County, so whatever was being said inside the tent was strictly speaking, no business of mine.

While I waited, several small children emerged from a tent. They crowded around and I passed the time asking and answering questions, clowning and making faces. About half an hour later, Jerry came out and motioned me back to the car. He said that the SNCCers, as he'd expected, were leery of Movement whites. We drove back towards home.

As we were pulling into town, the car began to lose power and speed. Worse, what appeared to be a police car was following behind. I steered the slowing clunker onto a side street and guided it to the curb. Then I looked around. I'd parked on a white residential street and not one, but two cop cars were pulling up behind. In the rearview mirror I saw white men in uniform getting out of the cars.

That morning I'd put a celluloid button or pin on the crown of my straw hat. The button read, "Southern Christian Leadership Conference/ Dr. Martin Luther King, Jr." I pulled the hat off and shoved it under the front seat, just as two uniformed men appeared at my car door.

"Now just what are you boys doing here?" one of the paunchy lawmen said.

I glanced at the markings on his uniform: he was a game warden, not a cop!

But it didn't make much difference, I knew.

"Well, uh, you see," I stammered, trying to see my way clear. "This here boy, that's Jerry, he works for my dad, over there on a farm we've got in Greene County. I just went over to pick him up, so I can take him to the farm where we live, over in Lowndes," I said.

"Yeah, well, what are you doing on this street?" the game warden shot back, clearly suspicious.

"The car stopped on me. I think we must have run out of oil," I ad-libbed, not having the slightest idea what had gone wrong.

The game warden was staring hard.

I reached for my back pocket, took a couple of bills from my wallet and handed them to Jerry.

"There, boy, go get us some oil!" I said.

Jerry opened the door on his side and walked towards the highway.

The two game warden cops went to the rear, to confer with the other two lawmen, highway patrolmen, it seemed. The second of their vehicles shortly backed up and left. The game wardens sat down in their car and watched as Jerry returned, can of oil in his hands.

When we opened the hood, the wardens drove away.

Jerry discovered that indeed, the car was low on oil! He replaced what was lost and we safely returned to the ghetto.

I felt like a hero for saving us from arrest. But Jerry didn't speak to me for the rest of the day, and I don't believe that he ever spoke to me again, though for a month or two, we lived in the same house. He never asked me to drive for him again, either. He avoided me, staying silent whenever I was around. It took me years to understand why.

The Movement, in my view, was purely a war of strategies and tactics: all was fair, as the saying goes. No one ever said as much, but in the view of black cadre, the Movement's tactics or means had to embody dignity and respect, just as its ends did. I was a "cracker." I had called Jerry a "boy," a racist act. As far as he was concerned, I had demeaned him. Just as Jimmy Collier had been willing to go to jail rather than reveal to the police his Demopolis address, Jerry would have preferred risking jail to the insult that, however well-intentioned, I gave.

In the days when we were building momentum for the boycott of the downtown district, life assumed a routine. Henry Jr. and Henry Sr., also a cement finisher, would leave in early morning for a construction job out of town. By nine or ten o'clock, I'd be out canvassing with someone. I usually stayed out, on purpose, past lunch, until about sundown, supper time. Henry and his father returned in late afternoon, and following our suppers, several of us—me, Ruth, Linda Brown, various locals, Henry Jr.—would gather on Henry Jr.'s small concrete front porch, watching the traffic pass and waiting for the nightly Morning Star mass meeting to begin.

Henry Jr. was the star of these front-porch gatherings. His long ebony arms propping up his jet black chin, he'd peer out at the cars and comment on the times. But Henry didn't talk about current events. Newspapers didn't reach us—there was no carrier service on our side of town— and they couldn't be trusted, anyway. He didn't talk about Having a Dream, or anything as lofty as that. Henry didn't talk about the weather, or gossip about passerby, either. He talked about The Way It Is.

A lot of what he said, he delivered in the form of quips, stories, and jokes. The drift of his wisdom remains with me in a fictional anecdote that he referred to more than once:

"There was this little construction company, see, and they had to dig a ditch. So they hired a couple of ditch-diggers. The ditch-diggers were white, 'first hired', you know.

"They had a deadline to meet, and they weren't meeting it. So the bossman puts up a little sign, says, 'Laborers Wanted', something like that.

"These two black guys come along, they see the sign, they go up to the job shack. The bossman gives them shovels and sends them out.

"So they're standing there in the ditch, shoveling with the white men. The white men get to thinking. They go into the bossman's office and say, 'How much are you paying those niggers?' The bossman says, 'Sixty cents an hour, just like you.' The white guys throw down their shovels. They say that they ain't working for the pay that black folks get.

"So the boss, he says, 'Okay, I'll pay the niggers 30 cents an hour, and you'll get forty cents.'

"The white men pick up their shovels and go back to the ditch, just as happy as they could be!"

Humor is conditioned, like any taste, and most people haven't been trained to see whites as the butt of any jokes. But in Demopolis, even Ruth and I rolled with laughter when that one was told.

Our chitchat sessions on the front porch would close when the Morning Star began to fill, mostly with adults, even oldsters. The church, red brick on the outside, was built around a semicircular sanctuary, with a crescent-shaped stage at its front. The Morning Star wasn't well-lit, and it wasn't air-conditioned, either. People brought ice-cream-stick-and-cardboard fans that carried funeral home advertising on their back sides, images of Jesus on the fronts.

The meetings would begin with a round of Freedom Songs, sometimes led by Collier. Then Henry Jr. would rise to speak. His eloquence was natural, always entirely spontaneous and vernacular. He'd tell people about The Way It Is. He'd ridicule "Uncle Tom" and "Aunt Mary": "You say that you ain't getting in this mess, eh? Well, I'm here to tell you, Aunt Mary, you're just like me: you was born in this mess! If you don't do something about it, you're going to die in this mess. You're in this mess as long as you're black." The crowds would go wild with applause. "Amen!" "That's right!" "Tell it! Tell it!"

Almost every night, Henry would rekindle his central theme, from which he never strayed far. He sloganized it as, "Racial Peace Means Black Folk Get a Piece of House, a Piece of Car and a Piece of Job!" Henry was familiar with the voter registration campaign and he wished it well. He'd heard about democracy and elections and such, and he was in favor of all that, though he never spoke of seeking office himself. He was a unionized cement finisher: it was bringing home the bacon that he cared about most. The Movement, as he saw it, was one whose aim was to open the economy's doors. His message was a part of the new wave of the Movement.

The mass meeting built enthusiasm for a picket that guaranteed support for the boycott. A showdown had been set for a Friday morning. The turnout that day was less than we'd expected, twenty DYC kids and a half-dozen women, but Collier or Wells thought that the number was sufficient. At the Morning Star we made picket signs of posterboard, bearing slogans like, "Don't Shop Where You Can't Work." The women and kids rolled them into cylinders, then walked behind Jimmy, single-file, towards the strip shopping center just across the color line. I walked with them into sight of the center and watched as they took positions in front of the stores, unfurling their protest signs. Then I turned back to the ghetto to canvass for the voter registration efforts.

Within an hour word reached me: Collier and seventeen of the kids had been jailed. The prisoners were too many for the Demopolis jail. They were being taken to the county jail in Linden. Word passed from house to house.

The kids were in jail for three weeks before bail was made. At every door I visited, the residents of the ghetto, disgusted and just plain mad, asked about the physical welfare of the kids. There was reason to worry: on July 4, the kids started singing Freedom Songs in their cells. Sheriff's deputies sprayed them with tear gas. The gas burned their skin and eyes, raising blisters everywhere it touched. The prisoners' pain was felt in Demopolis. Within days, the ghetto solidified. No longer did one see people coming back from downtown, shopping bags in arms. Carpools ran to Uniontown every evening, and all day Saturdays.

The Linden or county jail

Chapter 4

George Wallace,
never can jail us all,
George Wallace,
segregation's bound
to fall.
—Freedom Song

ONE AFTERNOON, RETURNING FROM A canvassing foray, I opened My Dear's kitchen door and saw that nobody was home—except for a white man about my age. He was sitting at the kitchen table, looking through a stack of mail. He was clad in Bermuda shorts, a polo shirt, and brogans. He was not a tall guy, but his bones were big and his limbs were thick, his biceps and calves, hard and huge. Even his face seemed to ripple with muscle. He had a stringy strawberry blonde beard, and like me, a pixie nose. A purple beret tilted across his head.

"You must be Arkansas!" I exclaimed.

He rose from the table, shook my hand, and gestured for me to sit down.

"How did you get here?" I asked, having noticed no cars outside.

"I hitchhiked," he said.

"Hitchhiked? The white folks would run you down in a minute!" I said in disbelief.

He pointed to a briefcase that he'd placed beside the table, a gray Samsonite model with a steel frame and a plastic body. It was the only possession that he'd kept from his student past. Gray duct tape held one side of it together.

"That's where they tried that one time," he said. "They came cutting across the shoulder. I dove out of the way, into a bar ditch, but they got my briefcase. But that was months back."

We conversed, a storm of words. Arkansas said that he'd come from Jackson, Mississippi, and the SNCC office there, and that he was just

48

passing through. He intended to review his mail, find a place to stay for a few days, and move on, maybe back to Camden. I told him about the coming boycott and the line-'em-up-at-the-courthouse days, hoping that he'd decide to stay, but he didn't seem impressed. Camden showed better possibilities, he thought. Arkansas, I'd learn, was a man for whom there was always a more important fight in another place, just around the bend.

When I asked why he'd left SNCC, he said that Mississippi SNCC—he didn't know about Georgia or the rest—was no longer accepting white volunteers. He'd managed to stay in, he said, under a sort of grandfather agreement, but it didn't please everyone. He claimed that for other reasons he'd not felt comfortable with some of the staffers in Mississippi, so he'd decided to give Alabama a second look.

I tried to sell him on Demopolis again, but he wouldn't commit.

Then he turned back to his mail.

I asked what he'd received. It seemed strange to me that a man could wander across Dixie, expecting the mail to reach him by waiting.

"Well, at least this time there's nothing from my family back in Malvern," he said, explaining that when he'd been in jail in Camden, his aunt had written to say that he deserved the beating that he got.

Then he showed me a letter, from the Selective Service.

In those days, every male had to register with the Service at age eighteen, and the threat of a draft was real. The Service issued us cards, each with a number designating our draft status. Whenever there was a change in our residence or eligibility status, under penalty of law, we had to inform the Service of our new circumstances.

As a student with passing grades at his state university, Arkansas had been protected from the draft by a II-S deferment. But then he'd left school to join the Selma march. He or someone else had told the Service that he could be contacted at My Dear's address. In the form that it sent, the Service was informing Arkansas that he'd been declared delinquent for failure to respond to draft notices, and could be jailed any day.

I had already known something about the situation. A week beforehand, I'd run into a white man in a white shirt and dark tie, getting out of a plain white car in front of Henry Jr.'s house. He'd flashed a badge at me and asked my name. He was from the FBI, he'd said. He wasn't looking for me, he was looking for James Benston, aka "Arkansas." Did I know where he was?

"What are you going to do about that notice?" I asked Arkansas.

He leaned over and tossed it into My Dear's trash.

"But you can't do that," I protested. "It says that you have to check off something and send it back with them. You've got to let them know where you are, you know that."

He smiled and shrugged.

"They might draft you," I counseled.

"They already have," he replied.

"What are you going to do?"

"I ain't going," he said.

"What do you mean?" I demanded. Organized draft resistance was still in the future then.

"If it's freedom we're fighting for," he cavalierly said, "I'd rather fight here than there."

The rest of the day was a loss for me. I couldn't get over the casual way he had taken what I considered to be a life-and-death matter. I didn't know whether to think that Arkansas was crazy, or to admire him.

Jim "Arkansas" Benston on porch of a Demopolis cafe

The next morning Arkansas was at My Dear's house for breakfast. We got to chatting about plans, and I mentioned that I thought it would be a good idea to take out a mail subscription to the Demopolis weekly, which had no readers on our side of town. Arkansas agreed.

As if teasing us, My Dear said that its offices were downtown. I muttered that I'd look for somebody to send. It wasn't the boycott that stood in my way. I was scared to cross the color line.

"Nah, it's nothing," Arkansas said. "Come on, let's go."

I walked beside him, nervous as I could be. We crossed Strawberry Street, came into a commercial area and gazed around. Arkansas was still wearing his shorts and beret, and anybody who looked at us knew what kind of white folks we were. I spotted two white high-school-age girls on the sidewalk and suggested that we ask them for help. Arkansas made a quip, something about asking them for a date. We approached the two and I told them that we were looking for the newspaper office. "Sure. Just follow us. We're headed that way," one of them said. There was no disapproval in her voice, only something that was more like a tone of caprice.

We followed a few steps behind, down one commercial block and into a block that was vacant. The girls had said something about turning left at the end of that block, but before we reached it, a police car pulled up. In a flash Sergeant Johnson was out, his billy club raised in the air and wavering, as if his wrist was arguing with his brain.

"Wait a minute, you boys. Arkansas, you other thing, look," he said. "You guys can run around any way you want on the other side of town. But you damn sure better leave our white girls alone."

Arkansas and I broke out laughing. We couldn't help ourselves.

Sergeant Johnson raised his club again, stepping closer.

"But Sergeant, don't you know?" Arkansas teased. "Miscegenation is a crime in Alabama! You can't give us permission to commit crimes."

Johnson was livid, really beside himself. His club was wavering again.

"You girls get out of here!," he bellowed. "Don't let me see you hanging around these guys."

The girls sauntered off. We heard them giggling as they left.

"You boys, get back on your side of town," he said.

I promised that we'd do as we were told, and Sergeant Johnson drove off.

But before we returned to the ghetto, we made the left turn, found the newspaper office, and paid for a subscription.

The arrests of the pickets had temporarily improved my living conditions. With Johnny Ray in jail, I had a bed to myself. But there was no relief from My Dear's suspicions. When Johnny Ray got out of jail, a consensus descended on the house: that I should have been behind bars with the others. That the Civic Club was opposed to picketing by SCOPEs was beside the point. I could have gotten myself arrested. On the day following the picket, one DYC member had done just that. He'd made a picket sign and come to the Morning Star, where he told the church secretary to call the police. They came, saw his sign and took him to jail. I'd been there when this happened: why hadn't I gone with him?

The truth was, I'd thought about it, not only on that morning, but in the weeks that followed. I'd initially thought it irresponsible. If I went to jail, SCLC would have to pay my bond, and money was apparently pretty short: I had received only one paycheck or two, immediately after arriving. Nothing had come since then. I'd also thought of the voter registration work: who was going to keep it going, if not us SCOPEs? I'd talked to Ruth and Linda, who had felt the same. I'd also talked it over with Arkansas. "It's one thing for those kids," he said. "They need to be together. You and me, they put on the white side of the jails. We wouldn't be with them, anyway. It can be dangerous. There's always a couple of guys that the deputies can put up to giving us a hard time."

Of course, there was a difference between me and Arkansas. Going to jail was an affirmation of the faith. Arkansas had been in jail at Selma, and he'd been jailed during the spring events in Demopolis. His loyalty was confirmed. Going to jail was a baptism, and I was still unsaved.

Nevertheless, I had decided to stay out as long as I could. Symbolic acts didn't interest me. I wasn't afraid of the jailhouse, because I'd been briefly in a jail, the summer before, for selling magazine subscriptions in a town that had adopted an ordinance against door-to-door sales. It seemed to me that I had to be ready to go to jail, willing, too, but that it was Alabama's duty to put me inside. I didn't discuss any of my thoughts about jail with the Haskinses, but My Dear's attitude made it clear that, even before speaking, I'd already lost the argument.

I felt uncomfortable at the house for another reason, too. It was Julia Mae. I'd been distracted almost every day since she'd come home from college. She was my age, she was studying literature, and most of all, she was stunning. Julia Mae was tall, finely sculptured and thin, like a track star. She was every bit as lovely as Henry Jr. was handsome, and her voice was as sonorous, too. Though we said little, I detected in her a sense of humor about my circumstances, as if she knew what it was like to face her mother's scorn. One afternoon on my way outdoors through the kitchen I glanced to my right. Through a crack in the curtain that separated her bedroom from the kitchen, I saw Julia Mae. She'd apparently just come from a shower. She was standing, nude. The beauty of her figure overwhelmed me and I hustled away, like the Mexican peasant Juan Diego when the Virgin first appeared to him. I didn't want to complicate my life with apparitions of things that could never be.

I wasn't sleeping well. At night I'd get up, go outside, sit on the patio and smoke until I was exhausted or calmed. One night, probably just before midnight, the kitchen door opened and Julia Mae came to where I was, crossed her legs and sat down on the cement. In low voices, we talked for an hour or two, about college, about Demopolis, about ordinary things. She made no excuse for joining me and she was direct and focused throughout the talk. I knew that if I stayed we'd meet again in the same way. The prospect was more than I could stand: I wanted her, but things were complicated enough. I didn't get along well with her mother, who was sure to disapprove—and besides, Andy Young had warned against interracial love affairs. The next day I sought out Arkansas to see if I could stay in the house where he and Collier had camped. Offering some pretext, I moved away from the Haskins place.

Arkansas and Collier were staying in a sparsely-furnished, spacious white Victorian house a few blocks north on an unpaved street called Capitol in a neighborhood called Frogbottom. The place had a wide front yard, a tiny porch, and in back, a chicken house and a corn patch. It had no garage, because its owners, like My Dear and Henry Sr. did not own a car. The house belonged to Mrs. Lena Frost, a short, fiery, chestnut-colored woman in her late forties or early fifties, a woman whose face was punctuated by a long dark mole or birthmark. Mrs. Lena, as she

was called, was a practical nurse who hired out, usually to white pa-
tients, at the local hospital, which was segregated. She shared her house
with a rail thin, dark, older man, Mr. Jerry, a retired farmer who always
kept a wide-brimmed hat on his head and a leather band that bore an
amulet around one wrist, a dime that he'd been given by a witch in New
Orleans fifty years earlier.

Mr. Jerry and Mrs. Lena did not share bedrooms. Mr. Jerry slept in a
narrow rectangular room at the back of the place; Mrs. Lena slept in a
large, square, adjoining room, where in her spare time she ran a one-
chair beauty shop, straightening women's hair with greasy stuff and a
hot comb. Mrs. Lena and Mr. Jerry were married, but the arrangement
was purely financial, having something to do with his Social Security
benefits.

The Frost house had a wide, long kitchen, rarely used. Mrs. Lena
forbade Jimmy, Arkansas, and me to cook there or to use its refrigerator.

Mrs. Lena Frost, left, and Mr. Jerry Frost, wearing hat, at Morning Star church

Our turf, a long, nearly vacant living room, was floored in linoleum and supplied with a vinyl-covered couch, a couple of chairs, and perhaps a small throw rug. Its only other furnishings were a space heater, which gave off the sweet smell of leaking natural gas, and a mono record player with two 78 recordings by bluesman Howlin' Wolf and a 33 ⅓ record by gospel star Brother Joe May. For one guy with a briefcase and two others with duffel bags, it was okay.

When Collier or Arkansas were around, being at Mrs. Lena's was like being a freshman in college. It was as if I'd gotten away from my parents for a second time, learning about things I'd never known to exist. Being there also gave me the chance to see what bonafide Freedom Fighters did in their idle time.

Jimmy had stitches in his mouth when I moved in. They were result of dental work, an extraction or something of the kind, performed in Atlanta or one of the cities that he'd toured. There was only one African-American dentist in Alabama, and he wasn't in Demopolis, for sure. Removal of the stitches was overdue. One morning he mentioned the problem. Arkansas claimed that with a pair of scissors and needle-nose pliers, he could probably do the job. I was petrified. Between Mr. Jerry and Mrs. Lena, the tools were found. Collier, as brave as Arkansas, leaned back on the couch, mouth agape. The hard part of the job was cutting the threads; they wouldn't stretch, to let the scissors blade through. But after making the cut, Arkansas removed them with ease. I watched, nearly fainting and full of awe. These guys were tough, I told myself.

A week or so later, Arkansas spoke at a mass meeting. A fourteen-year-old girl whom he named—I'd never heard of her—had died under the July sun, "chopping cotton"—removing weeds with a hoe—for a wage of $2.50 a day. Teenagers and mothers worked in the fields around Demopolis, leaving home in early morning, coming back about sunset. They came and went in the back of trucks that contractors brought. The girl's death seemed to me to be just a part of the way of things, but Arkansas was enraged. "There's a System at work against us," he preached. "It's not enough to stop just this abuse or that. We have to get rid of the System that puts people to work for $2.50 a day." His little speech had drawn amens from Henry and the crowd, but it fretted me a bit: I wondered if Arkansas was a Communist, like Little Red.

One evening as he lay on the couch at Mrs. Lena's house, I noticed that he was reading a manila-colored pamphlet. On its cover in big letters were the words, "Central Committee for Conscientious Objectors." I asked for a look at the thing. I'd heard the term "conscientious objector" enough to know that it referred to pacifists who refused military duty, but I wanted to look into the "Central Committee" angle. I figured that I'd caught Arkansas studying directives from the Reds. After all, the nation was at war against Asian communism.

My confusion was thorough when I learned that the Central Committee for Conscientious Objectors was run by Mennonites.

Collier was soon called away on tour, and Arkansas came and went, sometimes to Greensboro and Selma. I spent most of my days walking the streets and canvassing with a young man named Charlie Saulsberry, a veteran of the Selma march and the spring campaign.

Charlie was a relatively big guy, nearly six feet tall, pudgy with a rounded face and woolly hair. His clothes, always rumpled and dingy, were two or three sizes too big. But he seemed not to notice. His speech was contorted, but that didn't make him shy. He couldn't pronounce the last syllables of words. "Registration," when Charlie was talking, came out as "registray" or with effort, "resigtraysha." He stuttered as well, usually at the end of his sentences; he'd start out blurting and wind up stumbling. Despite all of this, he was one of the most original and competent people I've ever known.

Charlie had graduated a year or two earlier, in the same high school class as Julia Mae. He'd been the class salutatorian, though how, I don't know: Charlie wrote just like he spoke. But he read everything that fell into his hands, and had been one of a handful of Demopolis blacks who'd tried to use the public library, only to be turned away. Had it not been for his disability, which local gossip attributed to a childhood fever, he would have gone to college. Unable to do that, until the Movement came, he'd simply hung around, educating himself as best he could. His self-education had led to idiosyncrasy, as it always does, and to a roundabout way of thinking that was at first heretical to me. Once, irritated with some argument of his, I'd presented him with the first lesson of logic classes:

All men are mortal.

Socrates is a man.

Therefore, Socrates is mortal.

"That's not true!" he exclaimed. Then he went on to say that while Socrates is living, we cannot know if he is mortal, though the presumptuous might assume as much. To be logically correct, he said, the textbooks would have to be rewritten:

All men so far have been mortal.

Socrates was a man.

Socrates died.

Therefore, Socrates was mortal.

Saulsberry was a gift to the Movement, not because he was a smart-aleck, but because he knew everyone in town, especially the old folks. He became the key to their registration, but he took on the task, I think, not so much because he believed that it would lead to change, as because he didn't have much else to do. It was a game to him, and from him, I learned how to play.

On our first day of canvassing together, we started in Elmore Alley, a place where apathy made it tough to get a response. Our second or third house was that of an elderly lady. No matter how many times I knocked on their doors, the old folks kept their distance from me. It was "yessir, captain" or "yessir, bossman" from the men, "yessir, Mr. Dick" from the ladies. But Saulsberry knew how to engage them.

"Mrs. Parker, you know me, I'm Charlie Saulsberry," he'd say. "We're coming around with the Southern Christian Leadership Conference. You know, that's Dr. King's organization. It's because, you know how it says in the Bible, 'the last shall be first, and the first shall be last, and the bottom shall rise to the top?'"

Mrs. Parker would say yes, of course she knew.

"Well, black folks are going to get to vote," he'd say with a chuckle, as if some great irony were involved. People laughed with him, every time.

Charlie didn't know much about the Bible, but he sure knew dozens of phrases, and he'd throw them in here and there until he seemed to be delivering a religious message. He'd mention Moses, and he'd mention Daniel, and he'd talk abut Peter denying Jesus thrice, an Uncle Tom of his day. Nobody can say no to God: that was his strategy.

We had begun working together in late June. Near the color line was a big Victorian house that served as the ghetto's old folks' home. It had a television set. Sitting in its dining room alone, we watched Lyndon Johnson announce the passage of the Voting Rights Act. The President said that he was immediately sending federal registrars to thirteen difficult counties, and he named them, one by one. Marengo was on the list. Ostensibly, this meant the days of literacy tests were over.

But neither Charlie nor I were elated. When Charlie asked me what I thought about Lyndon's message, I acceded to his sentiments. Alabama had been a part of the United States all of Charlie's life: its life was well-known, and if a New Day were coming, it could only start with a declaration—which Lyndon didn't make—that its life had to be refashioned, top to bottom: and not only Alabama, but the rest of the nation. Hadn't black folks been voting in Harlem for years? Weren't they janitors and porters and housemaids and menials too? The promise of a registration card, as Henry Jr. would point out, wasn't the surety of a job or decent wage, of decent schools or decent medical care or anything of the kind. It was a necessary, but far from sufficient condition for liberation from a racist order that encompassed everything, not just the mechanisms described in civics textbooks.

The following week someone came to Saulsberry with a flier that he or she picked up. Its headline read something like, "Civil Service Act 1234, Section. 567 (b) 8." The first paragraph of its text said something about federal personnel being temporarily stationed in specified counties to interview "qualified applicants for registration." Charlie's informant told him that a white man had distributed these leaflets on blocks near the color line. But the recipients didn't know what the fliers said. Charlie deciphered bureaucratese: the bulletin said that people could register to vote—without literacy tests and other formalities—in a room on the back side of the post office.

Charlie insisted that we get out a leaflet that people could understand. We composed a draft, which said something like, "Register to vote today! No tests! Federal registrars are at the Post Office." It included a crude map with an arrow that said, "Go to the basement around back."

But with Collier and Wells gone, we had no link to the SCLC regional office, where bulletins were produced—and we had no time for that, anyway. Charlie knew a man in Elmore who owned an old drum-model mimeograph machine, which he used to print funeral announcements. We dashed to his house that evening and though his charges were exorbitant, we paid. We sat with him until nearly midnight, turning out hundreds of fliers.

During the next two or three weeks, dozens of people registered at the post office each day. But the old folks still held back. Charlie developed a new trick. After he had explained the biblical Last Days, he'd cross the street or go down the block, picking the home of a person whom the elder trusted. Then he'd talk the neighbor into taking the elder to the post office—even though the elder hadn't consented. Demopolis, like any small town, was a place where, if one knew who could prevail upon whom, one could lever people into doing what they wouldn't do alone.

The registrars, whom we spied only once, gave people little slips of paper, showing their eligibility to vote. Charlie would ask to see the slips when we made our rounds. Perhaps entertained by his speech difficulties, no one refused. In his poor handwriting he began keeping a roster of those who had registered, and those who had not. But Charlie's own mother wouldn't go: she claimed that the Ku Klux Klan had announced over radio that it had planted live rattlesnakes behind the post office. The community's half-dozen Jehovah's Witnesses wouldn't go, because their kingdom is not of this world. But beyond these few, ultimately almost everybody went: we visited their doors until they did. In Demopolis, the campaign was becoming a success and in Linden, it picked up steam. Ruth Levin had been traveling back and forth for weeks, and about this time, at the request of its Civic Club, she moved there for good.

Rural Marengo remained largely outside the Movement's reach because we had no transportation. We did what we could. One afternoon I was canvassing with a DYC volunteer named Joe Nathan Grayson, a high school honor student from the countryside who was staying with relatives in town. Walking east on Jackson we had come to the stock-

yards. That day was a sale day. Pickups and cars had come from everywhere. Joe Nathan told me that both blacks and whites attended, and
that seating in the bowl-shaped auction hall was segregated. A railing
split the bowl and the races in two. There were separate entrances as
well. Whites came in the front door. Blacks had to use an elevated wooden
walkway that began outdoors, ran above a corral, then snaked inside.

I got to thinking. Removing the SCLC button from my hat, I proposed that we go inside. We had the leaflets with us. Distributing them
would help to notify people in the countryside, I said.

Joe Nathan wouldn't go for my plan. He pointed to the herders
working in the corrals with whips. It would be easy, he said, for somebody to stampede us into the corrals, or force us off the walkway. We
could be trampled or lashed to death, or if the crackers got mean, simply beaten senseless.

I wasn't convinced. I headed for the walkway alone. After all, I was
wearing my overalls: I looked like a farm boy. I followed the walkway
inside, alert to the shouts and the banging of steel gates, ordinary sounds
in a stockyard, now with a more menacing din. Inside, I walked the
length of the bleachers, row by row, handing out fliers as I descended.
One or two blacks tried to talk to me, but I moved on, too hurried to
chat. About mid-way down as I came to the steel railing that divided the
races, a couple of whites waved me over.

"Can I help you?" I asked.

"What are you handing out?" one of them asked.

"Ah, it ain't nothing," I drawled.

Then I turned back to my task.

A couple of rows later a group of whites—five or six by now—were
standing by the railing's posts.

"Boy, gimme one of those," one of them demanded.

"It ain't nothing. Just some machinery that my dad wants to sell to
these niggers," I said, pivoting to distribute another leaflet or two.

"Buddy, you'd better let me see it, then," the white man bellowed.

There was no ignoring that knot of white men. I shrugged, handed
the guy a leaflet—and beat a path out of the bowl. As I approached the
end of the walkway, I heard a whip crack. I jumped for the ground.
Running, I looked back over my shoulder. The crack was just a herder,
moving a cow along.

Joe Nathan and I hustled across the street, went behind a building, and kept going until we were well out of sight.

In early July, just before the seventeen pickets got out of jail, Henry Jr. had come up with a plan to keep the boycott hot: a mass march into the commercial district, for a rally on the town square. It was to be the highlight of the summer, the biggest action since the post-Selma marches of the spring. The kids from DYC, me and Linda Brown, even Arkansas spent fully two weeks talking it up. We'd knocked on every door in Demopolis, and even though we'd had to make multiple trips to some homes, we had told every resident about the plan.

Henry, who said that he was salaried as a field staffer, volunteered to lead the march himself. No other field staffers were in town, but supervisors came through all of the time, and they seemed to think that the plan was a good one. The action was called for a Monday. Two days earlier, on Saturday, I stopped by Henry's house and found him on the telephone, calling the press in places like Montgomery and Birmingham. I'd never seen anything like it. Using a list that SCLC had developed during the spring, he telephoned reporter after reporter, telling each one that big things were set for Monday, 3:30 P.M. He even told one of the reporters that Dr. King would be on hand.

By 3:00 Monday afternoon, more than a hundred of us were gathered at the Morning Star. A whole army of lawmen were already mustered on the parking lot of the school grounds across the street. We heard the clink and saw the glint of tear gas canisters as they were passed around. Apparently, the cops didn't intend to let us get far from the church. Parked beside the police cars were the station wagons of half a dozen reporters, cameramen standing by. Demopolis was fixing to blow, on TV.

But I was worried, and so was Linda. I'd stopped by Henry Jr.'s house on my way to the church and somebody had told me that he'd gone to work that day. It didn't seem right. The appointed hour came and went, and still Henry Jr. didn't show. I surveyed the crowd inside the church, 200 strong and growing. Most were junior high and high school girls, with a few adults, mostly women. Some had come from Linden, and some, from the countryside.

In an attempt to recruit more males, Charlie Saulsberry and I walked through the police and press line, into the high school gymnasium. The gym was packed, as Charlie said it would be. Twenty or thirty guys were there, playing pick-up basketball. Two or three of the pickets who'd gone to jail were on the court. I shouted over the rumble of bouncing balls, imploring everyone to join the march, but my pleas fell on deaf ears. In desperation, I began to preach from a Freedom Song, berating like Henry Jr. "Ya'll sing it all the time, 'Before I'll be a slave, I'll be buried in my grave, and go home to my Lord, and be free.' Now, if you can sing it, why can't you do it? You're going to keep on being a slave, just as long as you're playing ball when you could be fighting for your freedom." It was an arrogant, even racist little speech. It turned several heads, but nobody joined us.

We returned to the church. Inside, the kids were restless. They'd tired of singing Freedom Songs, the afternoon was hot, and they were ready for action. At about 4:00 or 4:30 Henry and his dad drove in, at the hour of their usual return from work. We could see them through the windows of the church. I rushed across the street and knocked on Henry Jr.'s door. Quite irritated, he told me that he wasn't going to lead any march that day. "Doc, I have to work tomorrow," he said.

Our leader was ducking out. There was no point in asking whether the decision was his, or had come from Atlanta, on high.

Returning to the church, I conferred with Linda, who agreed with me: no Henry, no march. But Arkansas had turned up, and he and some of the DYC kids wouldn't give in. While a knot of us argued, everybody else was singing Freedom Songs, but now, in a different way. The kids were singing even the mournful songs in voices of challenge. Some of them went to the open windows and shouted out lines like, "Ain't going to let no tear gas turn me around." They were daring the cops, whose mere presence was a dare to us.

Arkansas called for people to fall in line behind him, to start the march. A half dozen junior high-age girls stood up and followed, still clapping and singing. At the door almost everyone fell in behind, still singing. Looking over their shoulders, I saw Arkansas' band go down the front steps. I pushed my way through the crowd as it filtered out, and I reached the steps—about the time that the billy clubs began to flail. The attack didn't come in waves. Instead, it was like propellers on an airplane, a continuous flurry. A half-dozen lawmen had encircled Arkansas, and it seemed that they were intent on killing him. A few of his followers screamed and ran. The kids on the steps quit singing— they let out roars and insults, taunting the cops. I was afraid that the cops would charge. I hollered for people to move inside, but nobody moved.

Maybe half of us had brought water-soaked towels. The plan was to pull them over our faces at the appropriate moment, as protection against tear gas. I pulled the towel from around my neck, took it in my hand and began whipping the crowd. The kids turned silent, but did not move. Seeing me, a few others jumped to the bottom of the stairs, removed their towels and began beating, too. We broke the enraged spirits of the mass, and pretty soon, everyone was indoors again. People rose and spoke accusingly, but I stood my ground. We didn't want 200 people in jail without SCLC's backing, I shouted. "You don't call a march and then back down," they protested. The meeting broke up: bitterness, confusion and discord. The cops taunted us as we headed our separate ways home. "Hey, where's the march?" "What ever happened to Freedom?" "Where's Dr. Coon?"

Somehow, Arkansas had gotten through the beating without internal injuries or broken bones. He was taken to jail, charged with disturbing the peace, resisting arrest, violating a new city ordinance against public gatherings. Bond was $200, about a month's wage for a working stiff. Since Arkansas wasn't on SCLC's staff and hadn't been arrested in a sponsored action, I didn't expect Atlanta to help. People said that when he'd been in jail during the spring, SCLC wanted nothing to do with his case. But everyone felt sorry for him, or everyone who was still speaking, anyway: Henry Jr. wasn't offering any explanations, and the rest of us weren't asking. Saulsberry took the lead, suggesting that he and a few others from DYC go directly to the community for funds, door-to-door. I joined the appeal.

At the end of our first or second day out, I ran into dispiriting news. I'd solicited an officer of the Civic Club, who'd advised me to leave Arkansas in jail. "If you go asking for money like you're doing," she'd cautioned, "people are going to think that SCLC can't get them out of jail." I discussed the perspective with Charlie and Mrs. Frost and the others who were raising funds. Charlie didn't want to quit raising funds, and he made a point: SCLC already had a bad name, because Henry Jr., its local staffer and chief, had backed out of the march.

On what we thought would be our final afternoon of begging for funds, we pooled our collections at Mrs. Frost's house, only to find that we were $40 short. None of us had money of that kind. I hadn't gotten a check since the second week of the summer, for reasons that no one could explain. But Mrs. Frost believed that a neighbor of hers probably had money saved to pay rent. She went over to the neighbor's house and came back with a sock filled with bills and change. We walked down to the jail and counted out the funds.

Fifteen minutes later, Arkansas limped into the lobby of the small city jail, a free man. His face was bruised, and he didn't speak; Sergeant Johnson was only a step behind. Arkansas, Mrs. Frost, and I headed for the front door. Sergeant Johnson stayed with us. As we descended the shallow flight of stairs outside we heard the cop announce, "Arkansas, I'm placing you under arrest." The charge now was vagrancy. Johnson grabbed his prey by the shoulder and yanked him back up the steps. A new bond was set that evening, $200 more. But it was futile to launch a new appeal. That night, the cops took Arkansas to the county jail in Linden. A few weeks later, he was sent to a jail at Selma on a draft evasion warrant. I never saw him again.

A couple of afternoons later, walking down Jackson, I saw Henry Jr. sitting on his stoop, talking to a man known to me as an SCLC regional supervisor. I stopped to say hello to the visitor. He wasn't friendly. "There's a bus leaving about 8:00 for Atlanta, and I want to put you on it," he said. It sounded strange, but I said okay. As I turned to go, he added, "bring your duffel bag." That's when I realized that I was in trouble with the brass.

Chapter 5   *To Atlanta*

THE BUS TO ATLANTA WAS full. I spent most of the night standing or sitting in its aisle, thinking about what awaited me. I was to present myself to Hosea Williams, SCOPE's director, who, I presumed, would call upon me to defend myself against an accusation of some kind. Time and again, I reviewed what had happened that summer, and thought of what I might say. Perhaps I'd be accused of making racist statements: I'd plead the circumstances. Maybe I'd be upbraided for having tried to beg money for Arkansas. I'd take my punishment, in that case, uncomplainingly. There was nothing to say. Arkansas had been helpful to us, more helpful than any car thief, anyway. What worried me most was the order to take my duffel bag. I didn't want to go home and I didn't want to go to another town. Demopolis was where I wanted to stay.

When I reached the SCOPE House, Hosea wasn't there. I went downstairs, crawled into a bunk and slept. In late afternoon I took a chair outside of his office and waited to be called. A couple of hours passed. Office personnel came and went, but Hosea didn't beckon me.

Then a white man in his mid twenties came into the House. He was thin and sandy-haired. He sat down next to me. Like me, he was wearing street clothes, not a Freedom Suit. He was Pat Gandy—the Georgian staffer whom I'd heard about at the beginning of things, a man who had been a staffer for years, ever since the Albany campaign. We'd no more than introduced ourselves when Hosea called us to his desk. As we went in, two very dark middle-aged men in suits, preacher types, came into the House and occupied the chairs that we were giving up.

"They tell me you two boys are rebels," Hosea bellowed. He wasn't being cute, or joking. "Rebels. Well, I wonder, should I take you over to the SNCC House?"

Gandy and I shot glances at each other. Did Hosea know that SNCC was no longer accepting whites?

"Are they here?" Williams said, looking out of his office's doorway. "Why, sure they are." He waved to the two suit-clad men. "Ya'll come in here, I want to introduce you."

The two men came in. Pat and I introduced ourselves.

Then we all took seats in Hosea's office.

"Now, I'm sending you boys to Liberty County, Georgia, with these gentlemen," Hosea said, turning to Gandy and me. "You guys do what they say, and don't get in trouble. I don't want to hear anything bad about you."

And that was it. No hearing, no questions, no chance to defend myself. In a minute's time Gandy and I picked up our things and loaded them into the trunk of a late model sedan that belonged to one of the preachers.

On the outskirts of Atlanta, the preachers stopped at an integrated chain restaurant and bought supper. While we were waiting to be served, one of them told us a little about Liberty, a county that lies just west of Savannah. There were no big towns in Liberty. Its farms belonged mostly to blacks, and blacks were an overwhelming majority, more than eighty percent of the population, he explained.

"About eighty years ago, malaria hit Liberty County and wiped out all of the whites," the preacher said. "What this means to you is that there are no light-skinned blacks in Liberty County. We expect it to stay that way," he said.

About 10:00 P.M. the two preachers dropped Pat and me at the rear entrance of a big, wooden, two-story building. They didn't tell us where we were. The two of us entered the rear door of the place, which opened to a large meeting room. We exited that room and came into a big, sparsely-furnished foyer, and beyond it, into a cavernous dining room. We found an institutional kitchen at the rear of the dining room. Then we went outdoors, into a yard, and peered in the darkness. We couldn't see the profiles of any other buildings, nor any lights of town, only pine trees. It was as if we were on a great estate.

Pat looked back at the building.

"My God, Georgian columns!" he exclaimed.

It was true. The hotel-like building that we'd come out of looked like an ante-bellum mansion.

Perplexed, we went back indoors and up a staircase. A dozen dormitory-style bedrooms were on the second floor. We turned on light after light, looking for some clue to our whereabouts. Finally, Pat ran across a bulletin.

"Ah, Dorchester Institute!" he said, greatly relieved.

Dorchester was a school where SCLC conducted citizenship training classes. Its purpose was to school cadres from across the South in civic topics and literacy-teaching techniques, so that they could prepare their townsmen to face voter registration exams.

Pat went downstairs, hungry. In the kitchen we found utensils, cooking oil and a package of frozen potatoes. Pat put the potatoes on the stove to fry, then began rummaging around, exploring. I followed him, step by step. In the dining room we found a juke box. With a screwdriver or a knife from the kitchen, Pat pried open its money chamber and took the coins for himself. Then, as we ate, he began to explain how he'd wound up with me.

He'd been called into Americus, Georgia, about 150 miles west, a couple of months before. Americus was at the moment SCLC's hot spot. Staff were being pulled in from everywhere.

In Americus he'd taken up with a black girlfriend. When other staffers raised objections, he'd refused to quit seeing her. He was thinking about getting married, he said.

We had been sent to Liberty, he told me, "because we won't get in trouble here. Liberty County is what is called a 'low-tension' area. There's nothing doing here. This is a place where they send people that they're not sure about, people with psychological problems, SCOPEs whose parents are worried, things like that."

I was stung. I told him about our troubles in Demopolis, and said that I wanted to go back.

"If you go back, you'll get fired," he warned.

I kept talking, telling him everything that I knew about Demopolis, trying to convince him that I should go back.

"Well, what you don't like is SCLC," he said.

Then he explained.

"You see, SCLC has a strategy. SNCC and sometimes some of us call it, 'Local failure, national success.' What that means is that SCLC goes into a place, gets the existing leadership to back its plan, and then creates a crisis that will bring in TV and the press. When they do that, see, it puts pressure on the politicians up in Washington to pass the kind of bills that we need."

I was at last learning the basics, but I didn't like what I heard.

"Dr. King comes in," he said, "at the point of the crisis, to bring it to a head or to dramatize it. He doesn't stay there afterwards, he doesn't go there beforehand. That's not his role."

"Now, the trouble with the strategy," he continued, "is that it's just what it says, 'local failure, national success.' People lose their jobs, get evicted, things like that. They're left with cases pending in the courts. We do what we can, but we can't stay around forever, you know. The purpose of the strategy is to create a national atmosphere. We can't be 'married to the community,' as they say."

I was somewhere between tears and rage.

"It's like Selma now," he said. "If you go back there now, you'll find that a lot of people are disgusted with the Movement. They'll feel like they've been left holding the bag. They'll say, 'Where is Dr. King now? He's run out on us,' because they don't understand. We come around— the national office does—with all sorts of community programs afterwards, like the Community Center at Selma, trying to patch things up, but really, there's not a lot that we can do until things get better in Congress. The battle has to be won nationally, not on the local level."

"Demopolis," he concluded, "is one of those places, maybe like Americus, that we tried to develop into a national crisis. But you can't always do that. Locally or nationally, conditions aren't always right."

I protested that Demopolis still had potential, and that, even more important, the crackers there deserved to be broken. The town hadn't been integrated, everything was in bad shape, a fight had to be made.

"Well, then," he said, "Hosea was right about you. You ought to be in SNCC. Of course, you're white, so you can't be."

"SNCC," he explained, "they *do* get married to the community. They go in and spend two years—two years is what they're saying that you've got to stay in a town now—building up a leadership, from the beer joints and union halls, places like that. They think that the old preacher-style leaders are too conservative, and for what SNCC wants to do, they are. SNCC says that you've got to turn the whole society around, from the bottom side up. It's a radical idea. It takes time to do that."

Then he told me that the confrontation at Selma had essentially been SNCC's work. "They'd been there for two years, and to hear them tell it, Dr. King came in just at the last moment, stole the show away from them. They're bitter about it," he said.

I told Pat that I felt married to Demopolis and that I wanted to leave Liberty County.

"If I were you, I'd stick around a few days. See what they're doing here, if they're doing anything," he said with a chuckle.

The next morning we located a SCOPE, a male student from Pennsylvania who had a two-bedroom house to himself. The guy was a terrible housekeeper, but his house sat along a highway. Dorchester was isolated, so Pat and I moved in with the guy. That night I attended a mass meeting with him. The meeting was held in a country church. The locals were discussing the formation of a credit union. It wasn't a bad idea, I thought—but the SCOPE could have organized credit unions in Philadelphia's ghetto. One came to the South, I thought, to join a fight.

The following morning I told Pat that I was going to catch the bus into Atlanta when it passed along the highway.

"Tell me if you go," he said. "I'll have to call headquarters and they'll fire you."

"But I was thinking of taking my case to Hosea, to tell him what's going on in Demopolis," I whined.

"It won't work," he said. "You've got yourself crossways with some of the local leadership. That's not your job. Your job is to work for them. Hosea probably won't even give you a hearing."

"Well, if that's true," I told him, "then what I'm going to do when I get to Atlanta is catch a bus for Demopolis. I'll get back and get the locals to explain."

"Just let me know," he repeated. "I have to make the call."

About noon, the bus came by. I got on.

Pat's call had unforeseen consequences. When I got back to Mrs. Frost's place, she said that my parents had been calling. I got on the phone and to my surprise, learned that they were relieved that I'd only been fired. SCOPE's office had called, they said, to advise them that I had left Liberty County and that SCLC would no longer be responsible for anything I did. Their caller professed not to know why I'd left Liberty, or where I was headed.

My parents had thought that they knew where I was heading and they didn't like the conclusions that they'd drawn. During the few days that I'd spent at home before leaving for Atlanta, a letter had come for me. Its return address bore the initials, RAO, for Ruth Annette Owens, my girlfriend. My mother had remembered those initials. A week or two later, another letter came, this one from the University of Texas. Its return address was that of the Division of Married Student Housing. I'd written the Division when Annette and I had been dating. Alarmed, my parents had asked a friend in the Panhandle administration to match the initials with a student's name. Only one name had turned up. My parents decided that I'd left SCLC to marry a black woman, a prospect that pleased them no more than the idea that at the age of nineteen, I was thinking of marriage.

I soon visited a couple of the members of the Civic Club to explain that I'd been fired. They got together, called a mass meeting from which I was excluded, and discussed the affair. Henry Jr. didn't attend the meeting, which made two decisions: that the commercial boycott should be resumed and that SCLC should stand by me. The meeting drew up a petition which, over the next couple of weeks, between 150 and 200 people signed. It asked SCLC to reinstate me as a SCOPE.

To revive the boycott, Mrs. Frost called a new round of mass meetings at a small church on Ash Street. She could not match Henry's oratory and the crowds were half their former size. But good news pushed the boycott on. Within two weeks, a grocery store near the color line hired its first black cashier. She was afterwards afraid to attend the mass meetings—afraid that she'd lose her job—but she sent a word of thanks, sufficient to persuade us that the store should be exempted from the boycott. Nearly overnight, it filled with black customers. Then she sent word again, asking that black customers not segregate themselves in the line that led up to her cash register. It gave her more work than one checker could handle, her messenger said.

One afternoon a big package was delivered to Mrs. Frost's house. Inside was a roller-type mimeograph machine, with tubes of ink—the state of the art in those days. Linda Brown had gone back to New York after the stillborn march, and the machine was a gift from the tenants in her Harlem apartment building. Because Johnny Ray no longer seemed willing to participate in DYC affairs, those who were still active regrouped under a new name, the Demopolis Youth Organization. They put the machine to work, churning out leaflets about the boycott. The Movement wasn't as healthy, in numerical terms, as it had been when the summer had opened. But it was moving again.

I was in bad shape, however. I was without even so much as a promise of a stipend from SCLC, and was soon reduced to credit at one of the ghetto's little grocery stores, owned by a man who called himself a minister. I'd go and charge a loaf of bread and a jar of peanut butter. I got by on that diet, but it quickly got old.

I was also in Arkansas' shoes, but lacking his courage: if I were arrested, no organization was pledged to go my bail. The only felicitous note in life was that Collier was back in town, at Mrs. Frost's house with me.

Collier's salary was twenty dollars a week, but he was low on money, too. We'd at first been able to buy cans of food at the ghetto's corner stores, and from time to time, had been invited for after-church meals, but only on Sundays. One afternoon Collier, as if he'd discovered gravity, told me, "I know what we'll do!"

We took up door-to-door begging. Collier took his guitar. We'd pick a house whose inhabitants we knew. He'd knock on the door, and before anyone answered, shout, "Food! Food!" strumming on his guitar. We were never turned away, although quite often, people would tell us to come back at suppertime—or on Sunday.

The tactic worried me, however. We could have been arrested for vagrancy, had the police only known.

There were other problems at the Frost house that, as time went by, began to undermine my resolve. I wasn't adapted to the poor man's life. Bathing was difficult. We used the chicken house that sat in the backyard, as the Frosts did. One of its two rooms was covered with wire mesh; chickens lived in that room. The other room was enclosed. It was the bathhouse. Our procedure was to heat up a pan of water on the stove—Mrs. Frost allowed us to use the stove for that—carry the pan out to the bathhouse, pour its contents into a ceramic-clad large steel bowl, and take a sponge bath. The hot water didn't help much, though. Demopolis was a cauldron in summer, and in the enclosed bathhouse, one sweated as much as one washed. I came away clammy, clothes sticking to my body. Ruth clothed herself in a cotton dress, and bathed while wearing it, coming out, always, in a state similar to mine.

Shaving was difficult, too. Heating water was a hassle, and I had no mirror. After a few trials, I bought a can of depilatory powder, a sulfur-smelling chemical that locals used to avoid razor bumps. I'd mix the power with water until it formed a paste, spread it across my face with a flat stick, and wait while the chemical burned. The process left my neck and jaws red and tender, though it did remove facial hair. Being clean-shaven required preparation and fortitude.

I was lonely, too. Though I envied the apparent indifference to women that I'd noted in Collier and Arkansas, I couldn't muster it. A shapely sixteen-year-old nicknamed T-Tot lived in the neighborhood, a block away. Every afternoon, about the time that I could be expected to return from canvassing, she'd come to our block and put a chair beneath a tree on the other side of the street from Mrs. Frost's house, then watch for my return. After a few days of this, I asked someone why. "She has a crush on you," I was told. The next day I stopped by to say hello to her, just to see if the rumor was true. She invited me to her place, where only her grandmother lived, she said. I declined—for about a week. Then one night, knowing better in a hundred ways, I knocked on T-Tot's door. Within ten minutes we were kissing on the front porch of her house. I heard a rumble or a banging inside, then saw T-Tot's grandmother in the living room coming towards us, an ax in hand. She shouted something about "that white man," and I took to my heels. T-Tot survived our brush with her grandmother, and never sat waiting for me again.

Despite such discomforts and misadventures, in brief moments I was at peace. While walking through the corn patch between the back door and the outhouse, or when sitting on the back step at night, looking at the stars through the pines, or when watching a quiet rain through an open front door, I'd sometimes ask myself just what we were struggling to gain. Demopolis had a tranquil side when only its rustic setting was in view. One time I mentioned these feelings to Collier. It wouldn't spoil nature, he said, for Mrs. Lena to have an air conditioner or two. It was easy to see that he was right.

Perhaps a week or ten days after I'd told my parents that I was back in Demopolis, a letter came in the mail to Mrs. Frost's house. It was from my father, the first that he'd sent. Inside was a check made out for $15, and marked, "For a steak dinner." Dad didn't have any idea what life in the ghetto was like. There was no place where a steak dinner could be had. A small restaurant on Ash served fried chicken as its top-of-the-line menu item, but on the occasions when I'd been there, my budget had allowed me only a pig ear sandwich. The check enabled me to re-pay the grocer and start a new peanut butter tab.

About this time a hearing was held downtown. Officers of a com-mittee of the United States Civil Rights Commission came to Demopolis to hear complaints from across the region. This was the event towards which field staffer Jerry, who had been in and out of Demopolis—some-times staying at the Frost place—had been working all summer. Ruth Levin came back from Linden to attend, and Charlie and I decided to drop by.

The hearing was staged in a banquet room on the second floor of the Demopolis Inn, which faced the town square, in the commercial dis-trict. The Inn—I'd never been within a block of it before—turned out to be an old but well-maintained hotel, whose bellman and waiter I knew: he was one of the men from the Brickyard. On our way Charlie and I saw a crowd of whites gathered around the plate glass windows of a drug store. The drug store also faced the square, on the same block as the hotel. Charlie and I went into the drugstore to see what was causing the commotion outside.

Ruth Levin, an oversized staffer from a nearby county, James Or-ange, and perhaps two or three other staffers—all black—were sitting at a lunch counter, chatting nervously. The drug store's personnel had re-fused to serve the group. Its members had decided to sit-in. A couple of stools were vacant, and somebody in the group invited us to join. I don't recall what Charlie did, but I looked back towards the plate glass win-dows. Some of the onlookers had the look of hoodlums or Klansmen, the two types being the same. I asked myself if I wanted to risk a beat-ing or arrest for the sake of integrating a drug store, and unlike the brave Freedom Fighters who'd come before me—I decided not to. I said so-long to the group and went towards the hotel, a little bit ashamed.

I didn't understand much of the testimony that the sharecroppers and farmers gave at the Commission hearing, but during a break somebody introduced me to a reporter. He was from the *Southern Courier*, a weekly that volunteers from the Harvard *Crimson* operated that summer. The *Courier* carried Movement news, stories about arrests and boycotts and legislation and the like. The reporter, whose name I don't recall, was white, fairly tall but frail, wearing a sport coat, a dress shirt and a tie. The conference resumed as we were shaking hands, and a few minutes later, he got up. Through one of the room's open windows, I saw him go onto the town square.

"The Klan types!" I thought to myself.

I got up and followed his steps. The square was a grassy place, crisscrossed by sidewalks that converged in its center, where a statue to the Confederate Dead stood. A telephone booth stood on one side of the square, within a stone's throw of the drugstore. The reporter was making a call from the booth. I scurried over and posted myself in front of it, eyes alert to trouble. I was going to protect him.

Years later, I decided that they'd probably come because they saw me, not him, but come they did, a group of toughs, probably the same ones that I'd seen at the drugstore. They had parked a car at the edge of the square and came walking. Whether there were four, five, or six of them, I don't recall, but pretty soon they were standing in front of me. They were guys in their twenties, all of them stout, with thick limbs, but not tall. It was clear that I couldn't win any tiff with them, so I folded my arms and didn't answer their taunts of "nigger-lover" this and "nigger-lover" that. My celluloid SCLC button—I wore it still—was pinned on the breast of my shirt. One of them tugged on it. Then they began pushing on me. The next thing I knew, I was lying on the sidewalk, knocked down by blows to the neck and face. They kicked my rib cage, kidneys, legs. Then I saw feet flying, and heard car doors slamming. I got up, dusted myself and glanced at the telephone booth. It was empty.

I was enraged. Here I'd come to protect this Harvard boy—and had he done anything to help me? I stormed over to the banquet hall, saw the reporter sitting there, and—before I could accost him—heard the meeting's public address system say, "Would you like to testify?" Everybody's eyes turned on me. I stopped. The chairman, who was white, like all the members of the committee, again said, "Would you like to testify?" I looked around. Everybody was still staring at me. "Who me?" I asked. The men on the committee nodded. I turned towards the chairman, "About what?" "About what just happened to you," the chairman said, beckoning me to a table. I took the seat he indicated, in front of a microphone. The half-dozen men on the committee asked if I knew the men who had assaulted me, if I knew why they'd assaulted me, and if I'd informed the police. "About what?" I asked, incredulous. "To report the assault," one of the committeemen said. "The police wouldn't do anything about it," I told them. I was astounded: the committee was having me testify about the basic facts of life.

When the hearing adjourned, I collared the reporter and asked why he'd abandoned me. "You don't understand," he said in a lecturing tone, "My role as a journalist is different from yours."

In the years since, I have become a journalist myself, and it is my daily prayer that I shall never find myself in the company of colleagues like him.

As I was leaving the banquet room, one of the committeemen, a white Southerner, invited me to a cup of coffee in the Inn's restaurant, downstairs. I accepted, though I felt terribly out of place: the restaurant had tablecloths and place settings and luxuries I'd not seen for weeks. After we were seated, I asked the gentleman why they'd called me to testify. "We were watching through the windows when those men attacked you," he said. "Sure, we'd heard about such things, but to tell you the truth, I, for one, had always thought that these incidents were provoked." Because I knew my own people, I believed that he was telling the truth: brutality was normally reserved for blacks, and only blacks were witness to it. But on the other hand, I felt that the Commission's work in eradicating discrimination was doomed if it was entrusted to innocents like him. Soon I politely took my leave.

When I arrived back at Mrs. Frost's house, Ruth Levin was there. The sit-in, she said, had ended in a victory of kinds. They group had finally been served, but on paper, not ceramic plates. The crackers had decided to obey the law in their own crafty way.

A few days later Charlie came to Mrs. Frost's house with exciting news. Somebody had given him a copy of *Jet*, a pocket-sized national magazine for blacks that, in Demopolis, circulated only by mail. A short bulletin entitled "Negro Sells 'Peace' in Race-Torn Alabama Town," told us something that we didn't know. Its text read:

White, Demopolis, Ala., city councilman John Coleman called it "black-mail, pure and simple." But Jacob James Israel, a husky Negro in his 40's, de-clares, ". . .it is not blackmail. I'm offering a service to those communities and I don't like violence." Both men were referring to the unusual activities of Israel, who admits he offers his public relations services (tries to quell unrest) in ra-cially-torn Southern communities for a price. Coleman said Israel asked the Demopolis city council for $5,000 and, when it balked, $3,000 to negotiate peace between demonstrating Negroes and the rest of the community. The council turned him down flat. But 15 local businessmen raised $1,500 as a down pay-ment to Israel with a promise to pay the additional $1,500 in the fall.

The bulletin was without attribution. Paging through the Demopolis newspapers that Arkansas and I had sent to My Dear's House, Charlie had also found a tiny, tantalizing ad placed in the newspaper by a jew-elry store. Its text read:

This is in answer to the many questions by our friends and loyal custom-ers. We have built our business based on honesty, quality and service to the people. We have no quarrel with those merchants who contributed to the $100 deal, but we want our customers to know that we did not participate.

Charlie was quite sure that these signs pointed to Henry Jr. He had sold out the boycott, Charlie said. There was another sign, too, he re-minded me. In early July I'd called SCOPE about my checks, which were directed to My Dear's house. The office had told me that checks were being issued regularly. If they weren't arriving, well, that was a problem that I'd have to take care of myself. Charlie thought that they were be-ing withheld at the Haskins house.

But nothing was certain. We had no proof and I had a doubt or two; I still do not know the whole story. It could have been that Israel had learned that we'd canceled the march, and was merely boasting about having made a buy, hoping to attract money in other boycotted towns. It could also have been that, overwhelmed by bail bondsmen's fees, SCLC had told Henry to call off the march, and to take the heat himself, so that people wouldn't think that "SCLC can't get them out of jail," as the Civic Club members had warned.

In any case, the Movement could be slowed, perhaps, but couldn't be stopped by bribery or bureaucracy or anything else: it had a life of its own, stronger than leadership. Indeed, the boycott had gained strength, despite its lack of charismatic leadership. As for my checks, the conversation with Hosea over the car thief had made my status clear: I had not been invited into the Movement to impute malfeasance to anybody. As Hosea would have said, "there are already too many folks in Dixie who are accused of that."

SCLC had scheduled a staff meeting in Birmingham, Charlie said, and he thought that the two of us should go despite my clouded status. I considered the proposal and decided that there was nothing to lose. A couple of days later we caught a ride with a local. Charlie brought his copy of *Jet* along, just in case. We arrived in Birmingham in early afternoon, the day before the meeting, which was set for the Sixteenth Street Baptist Church, site of the 1963 bombing which killed four little girls. We found the church, in the heart of the ghetto, and looked for a place to stay. We didn't have five dollars between us. King and his aides were at the comfy, black-owned Gaston Motel, nearby—also a bombing target during the campaign of 1963. Staffers that we ran into were staying at a slum residential hotel a block or two away. Charlie and I stood in its lobby as residents began to trickle in from jobs. We asked them to let us sleep in their rooms. One man offered to share his quarters with me and persuaded an uncle, who also lived in the hotel, to give floor space to Charlie.

My host was an ebony guy of average proportions, in his late twenties. He wore the uniform of a gas station pump jockey. His hair was prepared in a "process" or "conk," a style popular among lumpen elements and musicians. His room, on an upper floor, contained only a bed and a chest of drawers, but he had added a large throw rug, on which I was to sleep. After a few words with me, he left the room, saying that he'd be back about sundown. But he was knocking on the door within fifteen minutes. When I answered, he said that he wanted to loan the room to a friend who needed a place to bed a woman. I went to the lobby and about forty-five minutes later, my host came by, saying that I could return.

About sundown he reappeared, to put some cologne on his face and invite me to dinner. We went to an L-shaped two-room restaurant on the corner of the block. After we'd taken seats in a booth, two attractive young women in another booth beckoned to my host, who got up and spoke to them at their table. Then he called me over. Introductions were made. I returned to our booth, with him a few steps behind. Suddenly a man who was seated in the other part of the L came storming our way. He and my host met towards the middle of the floor. If anything was said, I didn't hear it. But I saw the other man's hand flying and I heard a slap. My host grabbed his neck; blood was spurting, as if an artery were cut.

I ran into the kitchen and out the back door. In the alley, realizing what an ingrate I was, I turned back. My host had left a trail of blood to the front door. I followed it outside and found him standing on the corner, his shirt covered in crimson, both hands on his neck, trying to stop the flow. It was rush hour. Traffic in the street was congested. I started approaching cars, asking their drivers to take my host to a hospital. Nobody would. After a few minutes an ambulance drove up, siren screaming. As my host was loaded inside, he handed me his room key and told me to wait for him. I forgot about supper, which hadn't been served, and went back to the hotel.

A staffer I knew invited me into its bar and I went along, although I don't drink. It was a narrow, dark place. People had to squeeze past one another to get by. While I was sitting at the bar with a soft drink in hand, an alluring young woman took advantage of the room's architecture to draw up to me. She put an arm around my neck. We stared at each other from a distance of inches, nearly eye-to-eye. I told her that I was in the Movement, but that was unnecessary, I hoped: I was wearing my Freedom Suit. She told me that she'd participated in the demonstrations of 1963. I began asking questions about that campaign, but her answers were vague. Night was drawing deeper and the bar was filling with men in business dress. She told me that she liked white men and laid a hand on my lap—and that's when it dawned on me. The bar was an annex to the hotel, which profited from the prostitution trade. I kept repeating that I was in the Movement and when the young lady understood that I meant, "I haven't got a cent," she ambled away.

I went back upstairs and was lying on the rug, trying to sleep, when my host came back about ten o'clock. An emergency room crew had put two dozen stitches in his neck. I was the cause of the fracas, he said.

"Oh, yeah, why?" I asked. The surroundings had made me suspicious.

"Because I introduced you to those two girls. The guy got hot," he said.

It didn't square with me that a mere introduction could provoke attempted murder—was Birmingham as bad as that?—and I wondered if the young women might have been prostitutes. Nevertheless, if my presence didn't cause the bloodshed, it sure didn't prevent it, either. I felt a bit guilty for having imposed on him, but there was nothing I could do.

My host changed out of his bloody clothes, went to his chest, removed a three-inch pocket knife from a drawer and left again. An hour later he was back, breathing hard, as if he'd been running. "I found the guy," he said, handing something to me. It was the knife. "Get rid of that for me, will you?" I walked over to the park where the fire hoses had been used on King's demonstrators in 1963, and tossed it into a trash can.

Sometime the next morning, a dozen locals and probably two dozen staffers and SCOPEs gathered in the Sixteenth Street sanctuary to hear a few words from Dr. King. He spoke briefly and in a conversational tone about the state of the Movement. It was an unrehearsed, matter-of-fact, routine address, not the kind of oration that caused staffers to snicker and refer to him as "The Lord." Afterwards the locals and a couple of SCOPEs, me included, formed a line, introduced ourselves, and shook his hand.

That afternoon Charlie and I sat in the second row of a meeting attended only by staffers and the SCOPEs, who numbered not more than a dozen; most had already gone home. Presiding was SCLC exec Bernard Lee, a very dark, short, and muscular man from the Atlanta office. He was wearing suit pants, a starched white shirt and a tie.

"How many of you SCOPEs want to stay after summer's end?" he asked the assembly.

Only two or three raised their hands. I didn't.

"How many of you think that you can run a county?" he asked.

Again one or two raised their hands. I didn't.

"Hey, brother, how about you?" Lee said, pointing at me.

I squirmed. I didn't know if he knew about my circumstances.

"Can you run a county?" he asked.

I turned to Charlie, who nodded to me. I turned back to Lee.

"Yeah, I guess I can," I said.

"Okay, you, and you, and you, you're going to run a county," Lee said, pointing me out with the others.

It seemed that I'd not only been reinstated to SCOPE, but had been promoted to staff.

The meeting broke up after that. There was no discussion of what had happened in Demopolis, no requests for signing forms, no talk of a check. I wasn't sure that Lee even knew that I'd been fired from SCOPE.

On 11 August, blacks in the Watts district of Los Angeles rioted. There had been nothing like it for years. More than 2,000 National Guard troops were sent in. Thirty-one people, including policemen, were killed, and calm wasn't restored for a week. But in the black quarter of Demopolis, we hardly noticed. There were no news junkies in our ghetto, and when we heard of the riot, we were uninspired: there were no white-owned businesses on our side of town, nothing to burn except, perhaps, the stockyards.

Watts sounded an alarm in white Dixie. The sheriff of Dallas County—Selma was the county seat—had long before recruited a posse of more than a hundred men, pledged to win any racial war. On Saturday nights, its members drilled on the streets of Selma's downtown. A machine-gun nest was built on a roof of a theater: Main Street would never fall! The trouble in Watts made Selma's posse look sane, and across the South, salesmen representing companies that made tear gas, shotguns, and other police gear had a field day. Reactionary whites were getting ready for a last stand.

Meanwhile, I was trying to ready myself for something that didn't make sense. Being on staff meant that I would be in charge of Marengo County. That didn't seem possible: how could I do that while Henry's relationship to the Movement was unclear? He was, after all, still the head of the Civic Club. How could an SCLC-sponsored Movement cross a leader who had been so important to its effort? Nothing was clear.

I figured that within a few weeks, I'd be told to leave Demopolis. But I didn't want to go anywhere else. The idea of meeting new faces and a new set of difficult circumstances discouraged me. Not only did I not feel portable, I didn't feel competent. "Running a county" anywhere else was more than I could do. It would take experience that I didn't have, and beyond that, a faith in SCLC's strategy and leadership. "Local failure, national success" seemed like a duplicitous strategy to me, and having never experienced American corporate or bureaucratic hierarchy, I didn't know that, practically speaking, the bosses are always wrong—and despite that, things get done.

My orders from SCLC soon came, and they were not as disappointing as I'd feared. A form came in the mail, saying a dozen staffers had been chosen to attend an annual two-week retreat with Dr. King at a camp in Frogmore, South Carolina. My name was on the list. Without any money, I didn't know how I'd reach Frogmore, but the meeting was more than a month away, and I had faith that like my other financial problems, this one, too, would take care of itself.

But about the time that the notice from SCLC came, I also received a call from my father. He demanded that I return home to college. I told him that I wasn't going to do that, and that I especially wasn't going to Panhandle A&M. Always the negotiator, Dad had asked if I wouldn't come home "just to talk about your plans." I'd promised to think about it. Going back to college offered me an exit from my straits in Demopolis and SCLC, but I didn't know if I should take it.

A few days latter, a letter from Dad arrived at Mrs. Frost's house. It contained a check for forty dollars, marked, "For bus fare." I decided to buy the ticket, maybe to return to Demopolis after the visit home, maybe not. Joe Nathan Grayson came by Mrs. Frost's house the following morning, but instead of going to canvass, we headed towards the bus station, which lay on the white side of town. As we rounded the corner at Ash, a police car pulled up to the sidewalk.

We kept walking.

"Hey, boy!" a voice called out. It was Sergeant Johnson.

We kept walking. Neither of us were "boys".

"Hey, boy!" Sergeant Johnson repeated.

We kept walking.

We heard a car door slam. I looked around and there was Johnson, his billy club raised, trotting to catch up with us.

"Dammit, when I call you, you better stop!" he hollered.

"I ain't no boy," Joe Nathan blurted.

"Shut up, nigger. I ain't talking to you," Johnson spat.

"Well, Sergeant Johnson, I ain't 'boy' either," I said, as calmly as I could.

"You, Reavis, get in the car," he ordered. "The chief wants to talk to you."

I got into the back seat of the vehicle and we pulled away, leaving Joe Nathan standing on the sidewalk.

At the jail, Sergeant Johnson ushered me into Chief Cooper's office, a small place, I thought, smaller than an ordinary bedroom. It was cool inside, thanks to air conditioning. Plaques and photos of men in uniform hung on the paneled walls. Johnson was standing beside me when Chief Cooper came in.

"Reavis, take a seat," the Chief said in his authoritative way, pointing to a chair in front of his desk.

The Chief sat down, too.

Sergeant Johnson took a position at the Chief's left shoulder, between him and the door.

"Okay, Reavis, you know about what happened in Watts," the Chief said.

I nodded, not knowing what he was driving at.

"Maybe you don't know, but there's people here who's plenty upset."

He went on to tell me about the posse's maneuvers in Selma, and about preparations elsewhere. "We spent $7,000 in Demopolis on overtime and tear gas during all of that trouble that ya'll caused last spring," he informed me. "And we want to know if you're planning something now."

I nearly laughed because I felt almost powerful. Restraining my giddiness, I told him that we were a non-violent movement, with no aims of rioting in any way.

"Oh, yeah, well if you think that, then tell me, what *are* you planning to do?" he asked.

"I don't now what you mean," I stammered.

"What are ya'll planning? It's that simple, boy! How are you going to make trouble next, what have you got in mind?"

"Well, I wouldn't know about that. There haven't been any mass meetings for the last few days," I said, buying time. I certainly wasn't going to tell him that I might be going home.

"Dammit, what were you planning before that?" he demanded.

"You ought to know, you've got spies in the mass meetings," I muttered, not wanting to confess that our Movement was rife with internal discord.

"Come on, Reavis," he said. He seemed to have lightened up, as if we were playing a game. "If you did know, would you tell me, then?"

I paused for a minute, to think how I should answer: how the Movement would want me to answer.

"Nope," I dryly said.

Chief Cooper turned to Sergeant Johnson.

"Okay sergeant, you can lock him up now!"

Then he turned back to me. I was still seated.

"Reavis, I'm placing you under arrest."

"What's the charge?" I asked, a little shaky.

"Vagrancy," he grunted.

The Demopolis jail was a one-story, two cellblock-affair. One cellblock was for blacks—only a fourteen-year-old was there—and another was for whites. The white section was empty. Sergeant Johnson escorted me to its furthermost cell, at the end of a hallway whose barred openings faced onto a paved street. I watched as he turned his big key in its lock. Then Johnson went away.

The jail was a relatively modern place with red brick walls, equipped with fixtures of mint green. My cell was about five feet wide and twelve feet long. Two steel bunks stuck out from one of its walls. On one of them lay a cotton mattress, about an inch thick. A rough wool blanket, probably an army surplus item, lay folded on top of it.

At the end of the cell opposite of the door was a steel commode. A steel sink was mounted above. The jail wasn't air-conditioned and my quarters had no shower—the same as at Mrs. Frost's place.

I paced, smoked a cigarette or two, and pondered what had just happened to me. I'd finally undergone the baptism of all Freedom Fighters, I knew, and I guess one could say that I'd done it my way: I hadn't volunteered for arrest, the inevitable had taken its course. But I wasn't proud, not in the least.

I was alone, frightened, and overwhelmed. My presence in jail—on the eve of a trip home!—like so many other things that I'd seen that summer, seemed ridiculous and mindlessly cruel. Life wasn't supposed to be like this in the nation where I'd been raised. It was supposed to be purposeful, to make sense in some way, and it was supposed to be prosperous, as nothing I'd seen in Demopolis was. The Movement, I'd begun to realize, was aimed at eliminating the indifference and the poverty—both material and intellectual—that was the scourge, not only of the ghetto, but of the whole damn nation. The job was too big to be done with the puny tools at hand—of which I was one—and indeed, the circumstances were breaking those tools. The System, as we called it, had broken Henry, neutralized Arkansas, and confused me. We had spent a summer with only one clear gain to show: a single job for a supermarket checker. The System wasn't winning every inning, but it was winning the game.

To ease my feelings, I began to sing, not words from a Freedom Song, but from a hymn of a different kind:

God bless America,
Land that I love,
Stand beside her,
And guide her. . .

But I didn't have the composure to continue. I threw myself on my bunk, and for the first time since I'd come into the Movement, I broke down and cried.

Chapter 6   *1966*

WHEN SERGEANT JOHNSON HAD PUT me into his car, someone at Mrs. Frost's house telephoned, not SCLC, but my parents in Texas. My father called Chief Cooper, and unknown to me, a negotiation began. Less than six hours after I was jailed, I was led down the hallway to the Chief's office.

"I've been talking to your dad, and he says that you were on your way home," Cooper said when I was inside.

"Maybe," I commented.

"Well, when you get to Lena's house, I want you to call your dad, " he said—handing me a ten-dollar bill. "Tell him that I gave you this."

I was stunned. Promising to repay Cooper, Dad had told him to give me the money for expenses on my way home. Their agreement was that I was to catch a bus within twenty-four hours.

The next morning, I was on my way home to Texas. Within ten days, I had enrolled at the University of Texas in Austin and found a job, shooting pictures of fraternity and sorority parties, my appointment to study at Dr. King's feet forgotten.

But I hadn't forgotten Demopolis. Shortly after Thanksgiving, I began organizing what I called the Demopolis Project Committee, a group that would return with me to Alabama in 1966. SCLC-SCOPE was planning a smaller effort for 1966, but I saw no need for the Texas volunteers to enmesh themselves in its maze. We declared ourselves independent of all groups except the Civics Club which—Haskins no longer being active—had invited us to town.

Our maiden effort was the recruitment of about a thousand books for the municipal library. The library was run by a board whose new chairwoman, the local newspaper told me, was the wife of the town's only white liberal, a Jewish haberdasher. Through him the Project Committee arranged an exchange: books for integration of the library that would hold them.

We delivered the books during Spring Break, which coincided with the first integrated political campaign in Marengo County. Mrs. Anne Braxton, a Civics Club leader, had placed her name on the Democratic primary ballot for the post of county tax assessor. The dozen of us who made the trip helped get out the vote, knocking on doors across the county, even in rural areas. Mrs. Braxton placed first in the primary because whites were divided and turnout was heavy by the county's newly-registered—federally-registered—black voters.

When the semester ended, a half-dozen of us piled into a van for our summer in Demopolis. The Meredith Marchers, who went from Memphis to Jackson, started walking about the time that we arrived. Three of us left Demopolis to join. Along the march, SNCC's Stokely Carmichael delivered the now-notorious speech in which he raised the slogan "Black Power," and in the days afterwards, we learned part of what lay behind it. Its logic, as far as I've ever been able to see, was patent. But to understand it, one has to know what was meant by "The System."

All civil rights workers, as far as I know, came to believe in something that we called "The System." Belief in the existence of the System became, I think, the key ideological point that held us together. The term was never defined in any formal way. It was not precisely the "system of apartheid" that the South Africans talked about, but it wasn't distinguished from that, either. It wasn't precisely the "capitalist system" of Marxist belief, but it wasn't distinguished from that. Each of us formed our idea of it only by piecing together things that we heard and saw; it was not an idea that came from texts or formal doctrine. The System was the rule of the people on top, all or most of those people being whites. In dozens of ways, the System profited by the oppression of blacks. Because blacks earned low wages, employers, mostly whites, earned fatter profits. Because blacks were disenfranchised, governments didn't face strong demands for wealth-sharing or welfare programs. Because the have-nots could not safely rally for democratic ends, society was run for the haves. The System thrived that way.

The idea was that the United States was not a democracy. It was run by the System, not by its people. This was, in essence, a revolutionary idea, swelling inside of an ostensibly non-revolutionary movement. In its latter years, when parts of the civil rights movement became known as the Black Liberation Movement, the idea of the System burst its reformist bonds, and the Movement became openly revolutionary. By then most whites had abandoned it, and the Movement's latter-day organizations, notably the Black Panthers and the Republic of New Africa, were repressed. The first expressions of revolutionism from within the civil rights movement came from SNCC, making their debut in the mass media during the Meredith March.

Carmichael and his allies began by pointing out that Southern blacks did not need sympathetic whites to lead them. If the role of whites had been to integrate the tally of missing and murdered civil rights agitators, they argued, the need for that role was passing, despite the killings of two black Alabama civil rights workers during the year that followed the Selma march.

Whites were needed, however, to take the struggle where blacks couldn't go, into white communities. The people who ran the System were white: that was obvious from the state of things. But the System didn't exempt whites from oppression. In fact, it used most of the American people against their interests. White civil rights workers perhaps couldn't do effective agitation in white communities like Demopolis, because we would not have been accepted. But we could agitate for racial reform in our home towns, and even if we could not do that, we could agitate against the Vietnam War, which was drafting inordinate numbers of blacks and disadvantaged whites to senseless deaths. The point of arguments to exclude us was that we were needed more among whites, where racism was stronger and the System resided. The System could be fought almost anywhere, and most needed to be fought in the communities—white communities—where allegiance to it was strongest.

I picked up only pieces of this message, mainly from overhearing discussions between SNCCers. Bill Moore, a quiet UT student from Houston, short and thin like me, picked up other pieces. So did Becky Brenner, the third member of our delegation to the march.

Becky was a petite, big-busted young woman with long black hair that hung below her shoulder blades. She was, among other things, the financial angel of our project. Though all of us had raised as much money as we could, she was able to supply whatever we lacked. It was she who leased our yellow Ford van, a vehicle big enough to carry the whole group. She had become involved after she and I had met in a UT classroom.

Becky had been raised in the Southern Baptist Church, and from that experience, I think, we shared, in rough terms, a world view. But Becky was less alienated from the church than I was. I think that she was motivated, as in many ways I had originally been, by an idea of Christian brotherhood that was broader than anything that was acceptable to white people's churches. None of us were accustomed to the radical racial and economic rhetoric of the SNCC cadre whom we encountered on the march—but what we heard seemed plausible, at the very least.

It didn't seem immediately relevant, however. We had made plans for months of work, and we weren't going to abandon our project because of any theoretical insight. Instead, after three or four days on the march—after, that is, sympathetic whites began to arrive on flights from Up North—we returned to Demopolis to make the best of our role.

Months earlier, SCLC had pulled all of its staffers out of Demopolis, sending them elsewhere: Collier and Jerry hadn't been seen since winter. Henry Haskins was attending a seminary, having left agitation behind. Mrs. Braxton's campaign for election had come to a bad end only days before we arrived. Fewer blacks voted in the runoff than had cast ballots in the first round of the primary, and she'd lost to her white opponent. The leaders of the Civic Club were bruised and were stepping back. Most student activists had criminal cases on appeal, from the spring and summer actions of 1965, and the handful who had been expelled from high school had been re-admitted only weeks before. Though Charlie Saulsberry could pull together a few volunteers anytime, the Youth Organization had ceased to exist. It was clear to all of us that Demopolis was not ready for another summer of boycotts and confrontation.

We found supportive projects. Becky opened a free day care center—this, in the days before Marengo's Headstart program—in a church that Ralph Abernathy had formerly pastored. Though the Food Stamp program did not yet exist, Bill Moore and Bob White, a hulking, bearded graduate student from Texas, worked with the Selma SCLC office to begin lining up people and paperwork to force Marengo into cooperation with a federal plan for distributing surplus commodities like peanut butter and cheese. A member of our group named Jan, a blonde who claimed to be a Rockefeller Republican, found two sisters, high school students, who wanted to publish a newspaper for the black community. With the mimeograph machine from Harlem, they printed a newsletter every week or two. It carried news of births, deaths, marriages and graduations—the sort of notices that white-owned Southern newspapers never published about blacks. Though he had to hitch rides from farm to farm, a volunteer named Phil, who came to us from a seminary in Philadelphia, kept rural supporters of the Movement informed about SCLC's move to combat discrimination in federal agricultural programs. I had planned to start a tutorial program in Spanish for local schoolkids, but held only a few meetings before the police began arresting me, over and over again. I spent a third to a half of the summer in jail, and much of the rest of it dealing with the consequences of my absences.

The first arrest had to do with the old vagrancy charge. After spending about a week in jail, I was brought into city court, for trial by the city judge. Don Jelinek, a thirtyish Manhattan attorney with the Selma office of the Lawyers' Constitutional Defense Committee, came to town to represent me. Only one witness was needed to prove the city's case, Chief Cooper. He testified that he'd seen me go from door to door, begging. The charge was, in a way, true: when Collier and I had gone knocking on doors and crying, "Food! Food!" we were doing just that. Cooper had never seen us, I don't believe, but we had long known that Cooper had informants in the black community; we just didn't know who they were. Cooper also testified that when he'd let me out of jail, he'd had to loan me ten dollars—didn't that prove that I was a vagrant? I don't recall if anyone testified for me, but in any case, the trial was brief: within a half hour I'd been sentenced to six months at hard labor. Jelinek demanded a jury trial, something that could be had only after my conviction by the municipal court. Bond was posted, and before long, I was at liberty again.

But not for long. We had rented a fifteen-dollar-a-month two-room shack, a place like those in Elmore Alley and the Brickyard, because we needed an office and telephone. I stayed there. The other volunteers of the Demopolis Project were quartered with families. A day or two after my release from jail, a registered letter came to the office. I signed for it, opened it, and found only a blank sheet of paper inside. It was a trap, one of Chief Cooper's gambits. The following day I was driving the van that Becky had leased when the police stopped us. They demanded to see my driver's license, which was from Texas. Then they told me that since I was a resident of Alabama—I received mail in the state—they were arresting me for not having an Alabama driver's license or Alabama car tags.

There was nothing that we could do about the tags, since the van wasn't ours. But as soon as I got out of jail, I walked to the police station to try to take the Alabama driving test. I was told that I couldn't take it; some obscure residency standard was cited. It was clear to me that we were boxed in. We would not be given Alabama licenses, but would be arrested for not having them. I called the group together, explained the situation, and told everyone that to keep matters administratively simple, I would do all the driving until we could litigate our status. During the next three weeks, I was back in jail a half-dozen times; Jelinek and Becky always bonded me out. Ultimately, the Alabama Department of Public Safety—headed by the notorious racist Al Lingo—ruled that we didn't need Alabama licenses or tags, and Demopolis dropped the driving charges against me.

An ugly incident took place while all of this was going on. A young woman from the Brickyard was walking towards downtown, her eighteen-month-old son on her shoulder. An auto with three white occupants pulled alongside, within two or three feet of the street's sidewalk. The white men taunted the woman, and one of them stuck an arm out of the passenger side rear window. In his hand he held one of those giant syringes that were used to put sulfuric acid into car batteries. He squeezed the bulb at the end of the tube, sending a stream of acid onto the woman's shoulder—and into the baby's eyes. Within hours, the child's eyes were swollen shut. Someone called us. Becky took the baby to a black physician in Birmingham or Montgomery, the first of two or three trips that she'd make for that purpose. Someone also gave Saulsberry the license number of the vehicle involved.

The next morning two or three of us went to the police station to demand that an arrest be made.

Cooper surprised us. Within half an hour, he had identified the car. He said that from our description of the occupants, he knew who was involved, three mechanics at an auto agency, members of the Ku Klux Klan. By sundown all three had been arrested—and had posted bond. The following Monday, the three pleaded guilty in municipal court. Two had worked out a deal with the judge: they would join the Army rather than face a sentence. The third paid a fine of some $400.

That, and two other incidents, showed me Cooper's attitude towards us, and towards the law. One morning a patrol car came to tell me that the Chief wanted to see me, quick. I went to the police station, where Cooper laid out a photo signed by George Wallace and his wife, Luraleen, and a couple of campaign posters. He told me that these items had been brought to him that morning by members of an out-of-town unit of the Klan. The party had visited, he said, to ask what his attitude would be if they were to kidnap me. "I told them that I'd pursue them to the ends of the earth to bring them to justice," he said. Then he warned me to be wary for a few days.

In a way, threats from the Klan were nothing new. On any night that we held a mass meeting in a rural church, the Klan came by, tossed bundles of *The Fiery Cross*, the group's newspaper, onto the parking lot of the church at which we happened to be meeting. Then they drove away; we never saw them. At the meeting's end, I'd usually go outside, find the bundles, and distribute the newspapers as people left the church. It seemed to me that nobody who came to our meetings was likely to adopt the Klan's ideology, and therefore, distributing the papers was a kind of joke. But the Klan's gesture probably caused some worry: if the Klan could throw newspapers, it could also throw firebombs. But nothing like that ever happened, and nobody tried to kidnap me.

Later during the summer, the group of us went to Linden to attend a mass meeting. I spoke there, and in passing, mentioned that Alabama's laws were unfairly enforced. A black man could be arrested for merely being on the white side of town after dark, but in Demopolis, I said, a police sergeant had a child, whose black mother he visited several nights a week. In my remarks, I mentioned the sergeant's name. As we came into Demopolis after the meeting, a police car with lights flashing pulled behind us. It was Cooper, steaming. An informant had told him what I'd said at the meeting.

"Reavis, I'm putting you under arrest for criminal libel," he said as he stood at the door of the van.

"What's that?" I asked.

"You said that one of my sergeants had a black baby over here, and that's illegal. That's miscegenation. You can't accuse a man of a crime like that. It's libel," he snorted.

"Is it libel if it's true?" I asked.

He stepped back, then chewed on his lip for a second.

"What do you mean?" he mumbled, as if, calming down, it had occurred to him that my claim might possibly be true.

I began explaining what I'd heard.

"I'll tell you what," he said after a minute. "I want you to go home tonight and write down everything that you know. All of it. Then you bring it to me, tomorrow morning, eight o'clock. Not a minute later."

I agreed to do that.

"If you don't bring it in, I'm arresting you for criminal libel. If it ain't true, I'm arresting you, the same way. I ain't shooting any paper bullets, now."

Again I agreed, but I was scared to death. I had seen the sergeant's car at the black woman's house but, of course, I didn't have personal knowledge of his business there. All I really knew were rumors, what people said. I was afraid that if I put those on paper, I could be convicted of criminal libel.

It was late, past 10 P.M., but I nevertheless telephoned Jelinek. He was calm, cool, smart. He told me to write down what I knew. "If nothing else, the chief may think that where there's smoke, there's fire," he advised.

I hardly slept that night. It took me hours to compose and type two or three pages, relating what I'd heard. With a trembling hand the following morning I presented the document to Cooper. He dismissed me. He did not want to read it in my presence.

Within a week, the sergeant was gone from the police force.

These incidents showed me Cooper's understanding of his role. He saw himself as being the man in charge of stopping or slowing the Movement. That's why he'd ordered the arrests on the driver's license charges, and that's why he had bent the truth in his testimony at my vagrancy trial. He felt that persecuting us was the duty of lawmen—but that it was not a job for uncertified racists, for Klansmen and the like. He was a by-the-book racist. Not all Southern police chiefs were so restrained, and the Marengo sheriff's office was not so restrained. I concluded that, under the prevailing political conditions, we were lucky to have Cooper as Chief.

Before long, Bob White took his turn in jail. He and Bill Moore, and probably Phil, were driving in a rural area when a couple of sheriff's deputies pulled the van over. Bob was driving. The deputies took him to the back of the vehicle, and, as Bob told the story, rather than mentioning supposed traffic offenses, they began to berate him because of his beard. "I don't even know what you look like. You don't even look human," one of them taunted. "Well, at least I don't look like a cracker," Bob drawled. With that, the deputy arrested Bob for "criminal provocation," i.e., for having provoked the deputy to think of assaulting him. It took us nearly a week to spring Bob from the county jail, and as soon as we did, we had to go back again.

The sitting county sheriff was being opposed in the general election by an independent or unaffiliated candidate. One of the background issues in the race was liquor. The South, including Texas, was spotted with what were called "dry" counties, places in which the sale of alcoholic beverages was prohibited. But even in most dry counties, it was legal to buy alcohol in a "wet" area and bring it home for personal consumption. Marengo was a dry county's dry county: regardless of its provenance, possession of alcohol was illegal.

Marengo's prohibition had three practical effects, the first and most important of which was the moonshine trade. People in the rural areas, moonshiners, made whiskey and sent it to distributors in town, called bootleggers, who sold it in Mason jars for fifteen cents a pint. Consumers sat on their front porches in the evening, sipping and chasing, a Mason jar of water on one knee, a Mason jar of colorless moonshine on the other. No one bothered them as long as they stayed in their yards. A woman who lived across the street from Mrs. Frost was a bootlegger, and at ten o'clock every Tuesday morning, as regular as clockwork, a sheriff's deputy came to her front door, to collect a payoff. Moonshiners and bootleggers who didn't pay were liable to arrest and prosecution. Whiskey was available only through an illegal franchise arrangement supervised by the sheriff's men.

Another upshot of the law was that it gave policemen and the sheriff's department an opportunity to collect fines on a grand scale. Half or more of mature black males in Marengo had at some time been in jail for drinking, and whites weren't exempted from arrest. Most of the whites who were in jail were there for alcohol offenses, too.

A third consequence of prohibition was that members of the Demopolis Country Club, on whose board the mayor sat, could not drink beers after their golf games, nor could they bring liquor to social functions at the Club. During the summer of 1965, the mayor had quietly begun lobbying to change Marengo into a county where liquor could be sold, at least in prescribed areas. But to win the campaign, he and his allies—a group that included Cooper—had to take on the county sheriff, for whom the trade in illegal alcohol was an important business. One of the opposition's maneuvers was to back the sheriff's challenger. Another was to quietly put into circulation petitions calling for a county-wide referendum on prohibition. The ally of the wet forces, on the black side of Demopolis, was Charlie Saulsberry, who was circulating the petitions even before I had left at the end of the summer of 1965. The white wets didn't try to woo Saulsberry, but blacks were now registering to vote, they could sign petitions, and the wets needed signatures.

Charlie decided to take the next step. Despite his speech impediment, he telephoned the challenger for the sheriff's post, proposing a deal: black votes for unspecified concessions. The challenger said that he was interested, and invited Charlie to bring a delegation from Demopolis to his house in Linden. The meeting was set for 8:00 P.M. on a weeknight. After making the arrangement, Saulsberry recruited six or seven supporters, and invited me and Becky to accompany the group. We left in two cars from Demopolis. I was sitting in the passenger's position of the lead car. Charlie was in the trailing car, sitting in the back seat, on the passenger side. The challenger lived in a house that stood on a corner. Our cars pulled up to a curb that ran along one side of the house, and Charlie stepped out. In the blink of an eye, a deputy's car appeared, and before Charlie reached the challenger's porch, he was under arrest. I flung open my door and accosted the two deputies who were handcuffing him. "What's the charge?" I demanded. "We're taking him in for 'Peeping Tom,'" one of them told me. Seeing that we'd been set up, our group kept quiet, and returned to Demopolis without knocking on the challenger's door.

A few days later, Charlie, still a prisoner, was brought to a Linden courtroom for trial. The sheriff, the judge, and his assistants began furtively paging through law books, apparently perplexed. This went on for twenty minutes before Charlie was called to the bench. "Charlie," the judge said, following the Southern custom of addressing blacks by first names only. "You were brought here on a charge of Peeping Tom. But we can't find any law against being a Peeping Tom. So we're going to change the charge to Public Disturbance. We'll bring you back for trial in two weeks." The bailiffs took Charlie away. We posted his bail, and through Jelinek, filed a demand for a trial by jury, a measure calculated to delay his appearance in court.

A few weeks later, the sheriff's department brought Jim Crow Justice to our ranks again. Mr. Peter Agee, one the leaders of the small movement in Linden and the rural areas, went to Washington, D.C. to testify in Congressional hearings about discrimination in the agricultural program. Agee was a middle-aged man, small in stature, and of very dark complexion. His tastes were formal; I don't think that I ever saw him without suit and tie, although he was a farmer. In Washington, a member of the Congressional panel had asked Agee if he feared reprisals from whites upon his return to Alabama, and Agee said that he did.

On the Saturday night following his return, he called us. Somebody, he said, had driven past his house and fired upon it with a shotgun. Nobody had been hurt, but he was afraid that the nightriders would make a second pass. All of us piled into the van and went into the countryside.

Agee lived in a three-bedroom, ranch-style house, an aged but well-kept place, indicative of his relative prosperity. When we arrived, we found fully a dozen people there, all relatives or neighbors, all men. They emerged out of the darkness around the place, all of them carrying shotguns or rifles. They had gathered to help Agee repel any renewed attack.

The men took us inside, and from closets and rooms, came up with guns for all of us. Despite the Movement's general commitment to nonviolence, none us protested or discussed the issue. We had come to help, and each of us took a gun. As a couple of us were setting up in a bedroom, Agee came in to explain what had happened in Washington. He told us that he had met Teddy and Bobby Kennedy and had been allowed to sit in John Kennedy's rocking chair. One of the Kennedys had given him a lapel pin in the shape of JFK's warboat, PT 109. He showed us the pin. Another had given him the telephone number of the Alabama FBI office, and had told him to call if he faced any reprisals. It was obvious that Agee had been impressed by the Kennedys, and wanted to do as they'd said.

I scoffed at the suggestion. The FBI, as far as I was concerned, was a part of the System: it had taken Arkansas away, and as far as I knew, it had never offered help to us with anything. But the others didn't agree. Bob White argued that we should call on Agee's behalf, and when I quibbled, he made the call himself. The agent to whom he spoke told him that what was happening in Marengo County was a purely local matter, out of the FBI's purview. We took our positions, but Becky and I soon changed our minds. We figured that the FBI would call the local authorities, who, if they found blacks and civil rights workers with guns, would arrest all of us. The others didn't agree, but Becky and I went into Agee's front yard, so that none of our allies could fire onto the road and the coming lawmen.

The FBI called the county sheriff's office, even though Bob had warned its agent that rumors identified two of its deputies as members of the Klan. Within half an hour, a deputy's car came down the road, lights flashing. It pulled up in Agee's yard, and two deputies got out. People hid their guns and came into the yard to see what the lawmen wanted.

"We hear that you've had some trouble," one of them said. "We want to take a look around," he continued, before anyone could explain what kind of trouble that we'd had.

Next to Agee's house stood a small white building with two rooms, used as a store. In the evenings, Agee sold soft drinks and soap and other domestic items there. Its front room was a service area, its back room, a storage place. The two deputies went inside, turned on its lights, and began rummaging around. Agee followed them, offering to help. I went in a few seconds after Agee.

The deputies were throwing things about, being quite rough. One of them said something about moonshine, but it seemed to me that their intention was to destroy the store, not search it—and it seemed to me that they had no cause to conduct a search. "Do you have a warrant?" I shouted.

One of them glanced at the other, and then, like football players moving on a signal, came to where I stood, near the door. One of them grabbed one of my arms. "We're placing you under arrest," he grunted, "for interfering with an officer."

The two manhandled me out of the store, up to their car. One of them called for back-up; soon, a second vehicle arrived. At that point, three deputies surrounded me, telling me to raise my hands. I did as I was told. One or two of them grabbed me, and pushed me, face first, towards a rear door of one of the cars. Then, as if he were patting me down, one put a hand to my pants, running it upward, hard into my groin. Then they yanked me back, and pushed me again. Maybe six or seven times they slammed me against the door. The pins that held my wristwatch to its band popped out, and one of my wrists started hurting. Finally, they opened the car door and pushed me inside. A few minutes later, the rear door of the other car opened. They had arrested one of Agee's relatives, too. The two cars pulled away, taking us to the county jail. No more shots were fired at Agee's house, probably because the deputies had satisfied the Klan.

I had been in the county jail before, twice, I believe. The city of Demopolis had a rule to the effect that no prisoner could stay in the city jail for more than a week or ten days, and on that account, I had been transferred to the county jail a time or two. Its interior was like the Demopolis jail, modern for its time, with cells of sheet steel and bars painted a mint green, and with commodes and sinks that were combination affairs, one-piece appliances of stainless steel.

But I regarded the county jail as a perilous place. In Demopolis, I had always been alone, the only white prisoner in the place, and usually the only prisoner in the place. The county jail, on the other hand, was always busy. Segregated jails were a danger to white civil rights workers because our cellmates often didn't take to us, and sometimes, jailers prompted them to assaults. I knew little about the fate of Arkansas after he'd been taken away from Marengo on the draft charge, but I knew that white prisoners had mauled him in the Selma lock-up where the FBI had taken him.

I had been lucky during my prior stay or stays at the county jail. Once, I'd been celled with a handsome young blond man, there on a liquor charge. He had stared long and said little. One morning after breakfast was served—a biscuit, a dollop of grits, a dollop of maple syrup, a slice of fatback, and a cup of coffee, always the same fare—I'd caught him staring out of the window before us, which looked onto the courthouse square.

"What are you thinking?" I'd asked.

"I'm thinking," he replied, "about my Dad. I live with him, just us two. We live up on a hill. The well that we use is downhill, about fifty yards. Every morning about this time, I go get water for the day because, see, my Dad lost a part of one leg. He's got a peg-leg, and he can't carry heavy things like that. I'm wondering what he'll do about the water now that I'm in here."

Later that day, towards sundown, he was staring idly out the window again.

"What are you thinking?" I again inquired.

"I'm thinking," he said, "that if Alabama was a horse, Marengo County would be its ass."

It's that kind of humor, I'd learned, that makes jail stays bearable.

The section of the jail that was reserved for whites consisted of two cells on its second floor. One of them, where I was usually quartered, was a simple two-man cell, up against a wall of the jail. The other, nearest the elevator, was a day room, a large cell with four or six bunks, a shower, and a steel table with steel benches bolted to the floor. On most days, prisoners in the small cell were moved to the day room following breakfast, ostensibly to use its shower. In Linden, the cell doors were controlled remotely. The jailer pushed buttons or pulled switches at the end of the hallway that ran between our cells and a window facing the courthouse. When the doors opened, prisoners in the small cell would step into the hallway and move to the left, to enter the day room's open door. Before entering, the small-cell inmates had to sweep the hallway with a broom that stood there. Once they were inside the day room, the jailer would close the small cell's doors from his remote station.

Sometime during my previous residence at the county jail, I'd also gotten to know a graying man whom I silently nicknamed the Gentleman-Farmer. His whole demeanor said as much. He spoke politely, with great reserve, never cursing, sometimes chuckling but never laughing. He did not ask questions, but answered when spoken to, as if he knew the world and all that was in it. He seemed to take part in any conversation merely to help its initiator. He wore the khaki pants and khaki shirt of his class, pressed and immaculate, as if he'd just landed in jail. But he'd been there for weeks, waiting for a "chain bus," a vehicle that was to take him to prison. His crime was moonshining. I tried to talk to him about the campaign to vote the county wet, but he wasn't interested. He had been in prison for moonshining before, he said, and he figured on resuming his usual life once again after an incarceration of eighteen months or so. It was as if he knew the risks of his trade, and could accept them without losing either money or social standing. He was calm, even serene, when he talked about his future. He had nothing negative to say about the sheriff, the deputies, or anyone else, including me.

I had been there when the chain bus had come for him. The jailer led the Gentleman-Farmer downstairs, where a prison guard took charge of him. The chain bus was a truck with ventilation openings, but no windows. I watched as the guard opened its back doors: wooden benches sat on both sides of the cargo area. Men were chained to the benches. The guard chained the Gentleman to a bench, and then, leaving the door open, walked around to the truck's cab. When he came back he held two packages of cigarettes in his hand. He hurled these one at a time into the truck, striking the Gentleman in the face. The Gentleman didn't smoke, I knew. Apparently, a state law required that each prisoner be supplied with two packages of cigarettes, and the guard had found a demeaning method of fulfilling the law. My guess is that as soon as the truck was underway, the Gentleman was placidly smiling again, offering his cigarettes to his new associates.

Neither the farm boy nor the Gentleman were in the county jail on the Saturday night of the Agee incident. A new crew had come in. The lights were out and it was nearly midnight by the time that I was booked.

The jailer was a man named Jimmy, fat and friendly, with a very slow drawl. As he led me to the control box that night, Jimmy said,

"Wa-ll, I'm gooing to put yooou with our niigggeer luuver." At first, I didn't know who he was talking about. But by the time the cells doors opened, I had recalled.

Bob had told me about John H. He was a muscular man of average height, with curly black hair and deep blue eyes. A regular at the jail, he was always in and out, usually for alcohol-related offenses. At some point in his life, he had borrowed money from black neighbors in the countryside, and the act had made him notorious among whites, jailers and deputies anyway. He had no political sympathies, but when Bob had been celled with him, John had treated him in a comradely way.

When the doors opened, John woke up, and mumbled something at me, probably something routine. I climbed onto the upper bunk and tried to get some sleep. Somehow, I did, until the doors opened again. Jimmy was putting a drunk into the day room, and as soon as the doors closed, the new prisoner woke everyone up with a bellow, "I'm the Alligator Man! I'm the Alligator Man!" At the time, a country song with that line was popular. The drunk apparently had snatched an identity from its chorus.

Again and again, the prisoner rattled the doors of the day room cells and bellowed, "I'm the Alligator Man!" I could hear the other prisoners grumbling in the day room. A couple of them knew the Alligator Man, and tried to calm him. But it was of little use. Once he quit bellowing about being the Alligator Man, he spent the rest of the night singing the chorus of a Merle Haggard ditty:

Tonight the bottle let me down,
And let your memory come around,
The one true friend I thought I'd found,
Tonight the bottle let me down.

At about 6:00, an hour before breakfast, everyone began to stir, having slept little and poorly. The Alligator Man was by now a bit more sober, and he began to inquire as to the identity of the rest of us. He stood at the bars of the day room, looking out on the courthouse; we couldn't see each other, but he knew that two men were in the next cell. Gingerly, I told him my name and explained that I was a civil rights worker.

"Well dude, I'm going to put you six feet under," he bellowed. "You see, I'm in the Klan."

A sort of conversation ensued, during which I concluded that he was not in the Klan—he didn't know details of its life—but that he was close to someone who was, perhaps a relative—that is, if anyone would have accepted closeness to him, or accepted him as family. He was still berating me when breakfast came. John handed me a palm-sized mirror and showed me how to angle it so that I could peer into the dayroom cell. I saw the Alligator Man, and he was huge, probably six feet tall, weighing 200 pounds or more, clad in jeans, like the rest of us. I was dreading the moment that I'd have to go into the day room.

When the doors opened, I stayed with John while he swept the hallway. We went into the day room together and sat down at its table, which had places for four. The Alligator Man was standing at the bars, looking out. He turned and began insulting me. I got up and backed off to the bunks, which stood against a side wall. The Alligator Man kept talking, inching towards me. John got up from the table and stood beside me at the bunks. The Alligator Man raised his arms, as if to lunge. John lunged first, trying to restrain him. A tussle developed. I rose and moved towards the two. Before I could intervene, two other prisoners leaped in, to save John. They backed the Alligator Man to the bars, and John and I huddled outside the shower, at the rear of the room. The shouts and bangs had rousted Jimmy, who came scurrying to the controls. The doors opened and Jimmy hollered for me and John to step out. Seconds later, we were safe inside our cell again. John had saved me from a beating.

John had operated a one-man television repair shop in the countryside. He was in jail, I learned over the following hours or days, because he had forged his mother's name to a fifty-dollar check, and also because he'd been arrested for "highway drunk," i.e., driving while intoxicated. One of the other prisoners, who apparently hadn't known about John's highway drunk charge, joined into the conversation when John mentioned that arrest. The other prisoner's story, like most of those told in jailhouses, was, I suspect, a bit fanciful, but it said much anyway:

"I was driving around the other night, with two of my buddies," the story began. "This deputy stopped us, because, of course, he knows all of the drunks in Marengo County. He had us get out, and he searched the car, and he found a bottle of bond whiskey underneath the seat"—

"bond whiskey" being liquor that is not moonshine, whose sale is legal in wet jurisdictions. "He told us that somebody had to claim it. We told him that the car wasn't ours, and that the bottle wasn't ours. But he said that somebody had to claim it, and that if nothing else, we had to flip a coin to decide who it would be. So we flipped, and the odd man out was me." His crime, I suppose, had been bad luck.

Later that morning, I told the others about Charlie Saulsberry's petitions for the liquor referendum, and somewhere in the course of my remarks, mentioned a run-in that we'd had with the mayor of Linden.

"Hey, dude," the Alligator Man joined in, "did I hear you say that you don't like the mayor?"

"I'd reckon that he's one of the reasons that I'm here with you," I said, stretching the truth a bit. The mayor of Linden was just another racist, and I'd spoken with him only once.

The Alligator Man then began to pour out a story about his impoverished adolescence. Both he and the mayor had attended the public junior high for whites, and the mayor had shown himself to be a typical, stuck-up member of the educated middle class. Poor boys like Alligator hated him. It was a matter of class, as far as I could understand.

I began to agitate, telling the Alligator that the System was using racial divisions to take advantage of all of the poor, with laws like the liquor prohibition. He listened for awhile, and then said, "Well, I don't know about all of that, dude, but maybe you're all right. I'll tell you what, you're the kind of dude that I think I'd like to see about six feet under."

The quip actually signaled that his hostility was broken. He kept talking about me being "six feet under," but gave me a nickname—"dude," of course—and kept talking. Within an hour, he was rummaging through his pockets—for political literature! He had brought with him two tiny pamphlets, which he claimed the Klan had given to him. He passed them over to me. They were tracts extolling "Big Jim" Folsom, the populist governor of Alabama, elected in 1948, when Alligator Man had been a boy. What the tracts said was that rich white men were using integration to exploit poor whites. I began trying to reason with the Alligator Man, and kept it up until evening, when Jimmy came with the news that somebody had posted Alligator's bail. My arguments, I know even now, had made little headway, because they said that class was more fundamental than race. If today, educated whites still think that race is more important than class, how was a backwoods redneck to know any different back then?

John H's trial came up the following weeks, and one of the final acts of our group was to attend. John's wife, an attractive, petite young woman, was in the courtroom, along with two or three children. We introduced ourselves to her, and she showed neither hesitation nor shame about chatting with us in public view. John had already pleaded guilty to the forgery charge, and had been sentenced to a year or two in prison. He was brought before the bench on the "highway drunk" charge.

"John, how do you plead?" the judge asked, using John's first name, because John was something of a regular in court.

He had no lawyer to speak for him.

"Well, judge," John began. "In the first place, I wasn't driving. The car was stopped. And I wasn't on the highway. I was taking a leak, beside the car."

"John, how do you plead, guilty or not guilty?" the judge insisted.

"Well, judge, it's like I was telling you, I wasn't on the highway," John began again.

"John, how do you plead?" the judge insisted.

John looked up with pleading eyes.

"Judge, does it really make any difference?" he asked.

Of course, it didn't make any difference. A deputy testified that he had found John beside the highway and found a bottle of booze in his car. John was sentenced to a year in jail for that.

Phil returned to Pennsylvania at the end of the summer, and the rest of us, to Texas. Charlie Saulsberry decided to go with us to Austin, where he soon found a way to survive, selling radical literature from a stand on the sidewalk outside at the University of Texas Co-Op Bookstore. A romantic relationship had developed between Becky and me during the previous fall, and in September, 1966, when the Demopolis Project was over, we were married in Texas. Sometime in November, a court session was held in Linden, with cases for Charlie and me on the docket. Becky, Charlie, and I returned for the trial.

Linden's courtroom was typical of those in the South, with high ceilings and a wall of windows with many panes in each. Opposite the windowed wall was a hallway, with two or three entry doors. At the front of the room was the dais where the judge sat, and to his right, the witness box. Jurors sat further to the right, in chairs surrounded by a wooden railing. Two tables sat between the judge's bench and pews for the public. One of the tables was for the defense, one for the prosecution. My trial on the vagrancy charge came first. Don Jelinek, the husky New York lawyer, came to defend me. He brought a witness, Albert Turner of SCLC, who brought with him a photocopy of the organization's payroll records from Atlanta. The prosecutor called one witness against me, Chief Cooper.

"I've never known the boy to do an honest day's work in his life," the chief said.

"Chief Cooper, you're a liar!" Becky shouted from the public section.

The judge instructed the bailiffs to seize her. "Mrs. Reavis, you're under arrest for contempt of court," the judge declared. Becky was led out of the room, off to the Marengo jail. The proceeding resumed.

Jelinek called Turner to the stand. Then he offered the payroll records into evidence. They would show, he said, that I had not been a vagrant, but had been employed, paid every week during the summer of 1965. The prosecutor objected. "The original is the best record. These purport to be photocopies, but we can't be sure," he argued. The judge accepted the objection, and it took only minutes for my sentence to be upheld.

Then the judge called Jelinek to the witness stand. In a brief proceeding, he questioned him about his credentials. Jelinek said that he had been admitted to the bar in New York, but that, no, he had not been admitted in Alabama, because a reciprocal agreement existed between the bar associations of the two states—there was no need for him to apply for admittance, he said. After giving this testimony, he sat down with me, to get ready for Charlie's trial.

"They were boxing you in for an arrest," I warned him.

"I don't think that they'll do that," the lawyer said.

Ten minutes later, before Charlie's trial opened, the bailiffs were called. Jelinek was arrested for practicing law without a license, and he, too, was led to jail.

Charlie was left without a lawyer. He said only a few words before the judge announced that he couldn't understand Charlie's talk. I volunteered to, in effect, translate, and the judge accepted my offer. He told Charlie that if he wanted a lawyer, he could pick one from the line of suited white men who were standing between the doors that led to the hallways. Charlie looked at the half-dozen men, some of whom smiled solicitously. He didn't want to trust a Marengo County white. The trial continued, with Charlie as his own attorney, and me as interpreter.

The prosecution called its deputy, whose testimony was simple: Charlie was a black man who had been found in a white neighborhood after dark. Everyone in Alabama knew that was a breach of the peace, he said.

Charlie took the stand, with me questioning him, as if I were his attorney. He tried to explain his presence in the neighborhood, with me repeating his words. But he could say little: the prosecution made successful challenges of almost all of his explanation, on the grounds of relevance.

Charlie, in a short summation, said that he had been invited into the white neighborhood by one of its residents, after all.

The jury convicted him.

Then I became my own attorney, in the charge that arose from the Agee incident. The accusation had been altered; I was now charged with disturbing the peace. The two deputies testified that I had interrupted their search of Agee's store. In cross-examining them, I established that only the two deputies and Mr. Agee had been in the store at the time.

Mr. Agee, in suit and tie, had come to speak for me. I called him to the stand. He testified that I had been on his property at his invitation, and had not disturbed his peace. In my summation, I pointed out that I had disturbed the peace of only two deputies, by merely asking if what they were doing was legal.

Of course, the jury voted to convict me. I believe that I was ordered to pay a fine. In any case, I was soon back in my cell.

On his belt, Jimmy the Jailer carried a ring of large keys, some of which, I suppose, fit the doors to the cells. But these were never used, since the doors opened remotely from a control box. The control box was opened with a large key, too. Whenever Jimmy walked, the keys rattled, and when he fumbled for the control key, the ring jangled even more loudly. We prisoners always knew when Jimmy was coming; he was like a goat with a bell on its neck. My arrival, as always in the county jail, was announced as soon as Jimmy and I stepped off of the elevator. Jimmy's keys said that I was coming.

John H was still in jail when I was brought in. His combined sentences were longer than the maximum time permitted for prisoners in county jails, and he was waiting for a "chain bus" that would take him to a prison farm. He had remained all of this time in our old cell, but when Jelinek was brought in, Jimmy the Jailer moved John to the day room, giving Jelinek the safer, two-man cell. Naturally, I was directed to join him.

Becky was housed on the second floor of the jail, in a row of cells on the other side of the control box. I discovered pretty quickly that by shouting I could make contact with her. My chief worry was that she would be alone, but she wasn't; a black woman was celled next to her. Becky was nearly jubilant, because her conditions, as she saw them, weren't bad.

Charlie Saulsberry was in the row of cells behind me, with several other blacks. Two sheet steel walls and a little hallway, apparently used for maintaining the plumbing, separated us. By standing at the back of the wall of my cell, I could sometimes communicate with Charlie without so much as raising my voice.

Jelinek was an olive-skinned man in his early thirties, ten years older than me. This was his first time in jail. I was looking forward to his stay, and tried to make him feel welcome, saying that the jail wasn't really uncomfortable and that the chitchat among us prisoners was a pleasant distraction. But Jelinek didn't buy it. He said that, first of all, he didn't plan to be in jail for long. He had called the office of fabled New York attorney William Kuntsler upon coming in. Furthermore, he told me, jail was a terrible place, with thin mattresses on its bunks. A long argument ensued, which showed me that even comrades in the Movement looked at life in different ways. Jelinek had conventional values. By then, I didn't.

While in college I had been deeply impressed by the doctrine of simple living advocated by Mohandas Ghandi, whose autobiography I'd read. As far as I was concerned, the thickness of mattresses didn't matter nearly so much as the content of daydreams. Jelinek and I sniped at each other about the meaning of life for five or six hours, until machinations from New York set him free. I am quite sure that the prisoners in the day room, who must have heard us, thought that I was crazy and Jelinek was nearly so for bothering to dispute with me. None of them ever said a word about it.

After Jelinek was freed, John and I resumed our routine of old, going into the day room for awhile each morning, then spending afternoons and evenings in the two-man cell. I had come to admire him during my previous stay, in part because John was a resourceful prisoner. Somehow or another, he had managed to get a jar of instant coffee into his cell. It makes no sense, perhaps, but coffee was contraband. We were allowed to smoke and have matches, but coffee was forbidden because our cells had no means for heating water.

Or, we had one, but the jailers didn't know. John had a little storehouse of contraband, all of it kept at the back of his bunk, under the mattress. Included were a couple of rolls of toilet paper and a tin cup. He removed the bedroll from his bunk, his being the lower bunk. Its steel surface was perforated by a set of half-dollar sized holes. The sheet steel had been manufactured that way, probably to conserve metal or to lighten weight. John took the cup, one of those brought to us with meals, and filled it with water from the cell's sink. He placed the cup over one of the holes, then rolled toilet tissue into a cone which he placed on the concrete floor, beneath the hole. When he lighted the cone, its flame burned upwards, boiling the water in the cup. We had coffee not only at mealtimes, but anytime we wanted.

A couple of mornings after my return, for reasons I don't recall, I wound up in the day room, while John remained in our cell. I was sleeping on a bunk that abutted the bars, and apparently I was sleeping pretty soundly, because I hadn't heard Jimmy's keys jingle. The racket of a rattling cell door woke me. Coming to, I saw a white man in a business suit and two white women, also formally dressed, walking out of the hallway, leaving our cellblock. The racket was coming from John, who was rattling and cursing. Jimmy let the three visitors out, then directed me back into the two-man cell, maybe so that I'd calm John. John told me the visitors were from the local welfare department. His wife had asked for aid, and apparently had received some before his conviction. But the trio had come to tell him that she was no longer eligible, because, they said, she had taken up with another man. The news completely undid John. He became a worried and frantic man.

John had always kept among his contraband a stainless steel tray, one of those used to serve meals to us. The following morning we took our turn in the day room. That afternoon when Jimmy the Jailer switched open the cells doors that led to the hallway, we returned to our cell, as usual—and then John moved quickly. He took the steel tray and inserted

it into the track along which the door to our cell ran. When Jimmy pulled
the lever or pushed the switch to close our door, it closed, but its bottom
edge derailed. By pushing on a corner of the door, John could pry an
opening, about twelve inches wide. He asked me to keep it pried open,
while he slithered on the floor—into the hallway. There, that first afternoon, with a spoon that he'd kept in his contraband stash, he unhooked
and unrolled most of the wire that held broomstraw to the hallway's
broomstick. He broke the wire by twisting it, then returned to the cell,
where we twisted it into two pieces, each about nine inches long. Then
he showed me what he had in mind. He grabbed one end of one of the
lengths of wire, and stuck his hand, holding it, through the bars. He
stuck his other hand through the bars and grabbed the free end of the
wire. He pulled the wire taut against the bar between his hands, then
began moving it back and forth. His theory, he said, was that with the
wire, we could wear through the bar. For the rest of the afternoon and
evening, he and I took turns sawing at a bar in this way. By the time the
lights were switched off, we had worn a grove into it, about an eighth of
an inch deep. That meant that perhaps with steady work for a week or
ten days, we could saw through a single bar. It might take two weeks to
create a hole a big enough to squeeze through.

The exercise in our cell was mainly an experiment. Since John could
derail the door, he had no need of cutting through the bars to the cell.
But in the hallway was a barred window, covered with a heavy steel
screen. If he could get the screen off, John said, he could saw through
the window bars and drop to the ground.

I didn't like the idea of an escape, because first of all, I didn't think it
would work. Even if we got to the ground, Linden was a small town. If
there was any bus service, it wasn't very frequent: how would we get
out of town? Beyond that, I didn't know how long I would be in jail.
Jelinek planned to appeal both of my convictions, and that meant that if
bond money could be found, I might be sprung at any minute.

I told John that I wasn't going to escape. Serving one's time had
always been a principle of civil disobedience, but my principles were, I
thought, more cunning than that. In the Marengo jail, prisoners who
couldn't pay their fines were credited with $3.50 for every day of jail
time. White supremacy had always been profitable for the System, and
I saw being in jail as an opportunity to decrease its profitability, by con-

suming white supremacy's resources. Keeping me in jail for the six months of my vagrancy sentence would cost the System about $700, and I was happy to be able to fine it in that way, instead of it fining me.

I might have felt differently had my sentence been faithfully enforced. Two or three black prisoners were serving sentences at hard labor, sentences like mine. Each morning I heard the cells doors open on the black side of the jail, as those men went to work at road maintenance. Each afternoon I heard them return. But no other white prisoners had been sentenced to labor, and Jimmy didn't want to integrate a work crew. Talking to the other prisoners, I gathered that it had been years since any whites had been sent out to work. I was exempt from the one condition of my sentence that would have allowed Marengo County to get any benefit from me. To the extent that I was willing to stay in jail, I was truly vagrant, truly a drain on the economy of white supremacy. That looked like victory to me.

Pondering all of this, I had become thoroughly content. I had done what my conscience had told me to do—I had no sense of failed obligation—and with every sunrise, I was making the System pay for its nonsense.

John's circumstances, of course, were different, so much so that there was never anything said about whether or not I'd help him escape. I had no choice: he was my friend, and as far as I was concerned, he was a victim of the System, too. I understood that if we got caught, I'd probably draw an additional sentence, but that was a risk that I had to take. In the frame of mind into which I'd slipped, a longer sentence meant only an opportunity to impose a bigger fine on the System.

The following day, after John and I returned to the our cell from the day room, he slithered into the hallway and with his spoon tried to undo the screws that held the steel screen to the window. They were Phillips-head screws, and the spoon wouldn't fit. So we spent the next day or two scraping the spoon's handle against the cement floor, forming it into a makeshift screwdriver. When that job was completed, John was able to remove the screen. He set it beside him and then began sawing on the bars of the window. The work was pretty hard on his hands, and we soon began taking turns. Whenever we heard Jimmy's keys jangle, we set the screen back in place—we didn't have time to screw it into place—and slithered back into our cell. Jimmy rarely came into the hallway, and didn't come at all during that time. Our project was known only to us and to the fellow prisoners who watched our work from the day room.

Becky's sentence on the contempt charges had been for five days in jail. When her time was up, she went back to Mrs. Frost's place, and before leaving for Texas to raise money for my bail, she came to the jail with cigarettes and textbooks for me. Jimmy accepted them, and brought them up. At the time I was enrolled in basic courses in philosophy, and among the books that Becky left for me were several of the Socratic dialogues. From their arrival onwards, my life in jail was nearly idyllic. I worked on the bars and read about Socrates. When I was done with a book, I rolled up its pages, two or three at a time, and passed them through a nickel-sized hole in the back wall to Charlie Saulsberry. We couldn't communicate at much length, because the acoustics were bad, but a couple of times we passed comment on what we'd read. We were students on scholarship at a university whose campus life was that of the poor.

One morning about two weeks later, I awoke to the sound of voices. Two men in suits were standing in the hallway. One of them was Dad; another was a lawyer that he'd brought from Texas. They had come to get me out of jail, they said. I paused a minute, trying to figure out how to explain and hoping that meanwhile, neither of them would lean against the screen that was merely sitting in the window, due to John's work. I told my visitors that I didn't want out of jail. Dad tried to persuade me, but that, of course, was of little use. He was displeased when he left, and he vowed to spring me if he could. My sentence on the charge of disturbing the peace, I knew, could be mollified with money. But I felt safe knowing that nobody could buy my freedom on the vagrancy charge.

A morning or two later, when breakfast came, we noticed something odd. We were given double rations: two biscuits, two pieces of fatback, two dollops of grits and two of syrup, two cups of coffee. For a moment John and I scratched our heads: what was this? Then we realized that it was Thanksgiving Day. At noon venison came with our meal, its source, no mystery to us. In the day room cell were two unfortunates who had been caught hunting deer without a license.

Meanwhile, Jelinek had been busy on Charlie's behalf. He was freed a day or two after Dad's visit. Dad and his lawyer rented a motel room in Demopolis, where the police tailed them, day and night. After several days, Dad and the lawyer negotiated a deal with the Linden authorities. It involved $500, to complete bail bond monies sent by the Unitarian-Universalist religious association, apparently in response to Becky's effort. They also paid $1200 in fines and costs on the disturbing the peace charge. Dad went to request a transfer of cash from his account at home, but Linden's banker wouldn't cooperate, because, he said, he wanted nothing to do with people like me. Dad got the money through a Western Union office, and Jimmy came for me.

Posting bond, as things turned out, was unnecessary. Jelinek had been busy on my case, too. He'd gotten in touch with Alvin Bronstein, a lawyer for the American Civil Liberties Union, who was preparing a case against Dixie's vagrancy laws. Thirteen defendants, through their lawyers, sued the region's governments in federal court, and a few minutes before he took me downstairs, Jimmy got word that the U. S. Fifth Circuit Court had struck down Dixie's laws against beggary. He had to release me. My standing as a rebel vagrant, both on the streets and in jail, was completely abolished.

Charlie and I went back to Texas together. I resumed student life with Becky in the honeymoon cottage that we'd rented for the semester. About a month after my return, I received a letter from John H. He had continued with his escape plan, he said, but had been caught, he did not say how. A year was added to his sentences for the attempt. His letter came from a prison farm. I mailed him a carton of cigarettes, but never heard from him after that.

In the ensuing years, My Dear Haskins died of natural causes. Henry Haskins became a big-time preacher in Birmingham. Mrs. Lena Frost was run over and killed by a car while she was crossing a street. Chief Cooper died an old man's death, and the Demopolis police station was named in his honor. Arkansas turned up in Chicago, where he was active in the Teamsters and postal unions. In later years he became mildly famous as a participant in Iron Man contests. Becky, Bob White, Bill Moore, Saulsberry, and I spent most of the remainder of the decade in Austin, assailing the System whenever we could. About 1970, Charlie Saulsberry went to California. None of us, and no one in Demopolis, has heard from him in more than twenty years, and he doesn't turn up in databases that I've checked. All of us presume that he is anonymously dead. In the years since, the town of Demopolis gave way to some of the demands and changes that the Movement made. Demopolis now has two black city councilmen and a black police chief.

In memoirs like this, writers sometimes discourse on the meaning of what they've seen. I was only a soldier in the Movement, not a strategist or philosopher, and my worthiness as an evaluator is limited. I think about the Movement nearly every day, and each January, when Dr. Martin Luther King Day is celebrated, I find myself wondering if the Movement in which I participated is the same one that the stylish and smiling television commentators are talking about. Where was I when the Movement won the struggle for equality, as everyone seems to think?

The important question to all veterans of the Movement, I believe, is this: which force was more influential in shaping the present, our Movement or the System? In my mind the answer is clear. The System made some concessions to our protests, but its power was never trumped. Marengo County inspired the nation more than anyone in the Movement did. The evidence is on police blotters and on the front pages of our newspapers, every day: America has a Drug War, patterned on Marengo's liquor law, and the nation is developing a pattern of income distribution like the duality of rich and poor that lay at bottom of Alabama's injustice. The System exists, even today, and I am sure that it will outlive me. During the brief span of Dr. King's movement, it lost a few hands, but it's still ahead in the game. But history has not ended, and deep in my heart, I do believe that we—'we' being virtually the whole human race—will overcome someday.

AFTERWORD

During the years in which I tinkered with the simple memoir, I got in touch, first of all, with Becky Brenner and Ruth Levin. When I had finished my draft, I took the unusual step of sending it to them. Both suggested changes that to the best of my ability, I incorporated.

As my editors at the University of North Texas Press were moving toward publication, they asked Atlanta author and professor David Garrow to perform the task known as "academic review" of my work. Professor Garrow helped me find Jim "Arkansas" Benston, who now lives in Colorado and is known by a new nickname, "Striker." Arkansas, as he'll always be to me, sent me a thorough critique, some of whose major points I could not incorporate. He told me that my chronology is off, that the real course of events detailed in this book should, for example, place the agriculture hearing on the Demopolis square after his arrest and disappearance from Marengo County. He attended that hearing, he says. And he suggests that my memoir will lose "credibility" if I don't reorder those events.

But I don't think that's the case.

I have attempted to record the problems, traumas, and hopes of our Movement; local historians may be able to put those very human intangibles in order, because chronology is a more serious matter for them than for me. The important thing, I believe, is to show the reader that our Movement was a struggle against all kinds of odds: poverty and the lack of organizational resources, inexperience, immaturity, residual racial distrust, and hostility, from both blacks and whites. While we accomplished some of what we set out to do, in the main, I believe that we were defeated, and that our hopes now fairly or unfairly devolve onto the generations that will come after us. My only hope is that in reading this work, members of a younger generation will see what I and my peers did not accomplish, and will do what they can for the cause— whether they pardon us Baby Boomers or not.

While rereading this memoir perhaps twenty times in the course of correcting errors in style, tone, and fact, I found myself sometimes buoyed by the feeling that in the days of the Movement, those of us who participated had good reason to live, and we lived our reasons. But most of the time I was saddened to read my own words. I am today a fairly successful person in my field of work, but when I look back upon my youth, I see that today, almost no one—and I include myself—approaches life with the passion and purpose of the Movement years. Our nation is passing through an era of complacency, and the relevance of our lives fades, like my memories, day by day.

INDEX